OF MOUNTAINS AND SEAS

山海经传

Of Mountains and Seas
A Tragicomedy of the Gods in Three Acts

Gao Xingjian

Translated by Gilbert C. F. Fong

The Chinese University Press

Of Mountains and Seas: A Tragicomedy of the Gods in Three Acts
By Gao Xingjian
Translated by Gilbert C. F. Fong

This collection copyright © Gao Xingjian, 2008
English language copyright © Gilbert C. F. Fong, 2008

All Rights Reserved. No part of this publication may be reproduced or transmitted in any form or by any means, electronic or mechanical, including photocopying, recording, or any information storage or retrieval system, without permission in writing from the authors.

ISBN 978–962–996–375–0

THE CHINESE UNIVERSITY PRESS
The Chinese University of Hong Kong
Sha Tin, N. T., Hong Kong
Fax: +852 2603 6692
      +852 2603 7355
E-mail: cup@cuhk.edu.hk
Web-site: www.chineseupress.com

Printed in Hong Kong

This work described in this book is part of the result of "The Gao Xingjian Project" which was fully supported by the Earmarked Research Grant dispensed by the Research Grants Council of the Hong Kong Special Administrative Region (Project no.: CUHK 4119/03H).

All paintings and calligraphy by Gao Xingjian
Courtesy of Gao Xingjian

Contents

Acknowledgements and Translator's Note	vi
Introduction: Purity of Origin	vii
List of Illustrations	xix

OF MOUNTAINS AND SEAS

Cast of Characters	3
Act I	7
Act II	35
Act III	77
On Performing *Of Mountains and Seas*, by Gao Xingjian	97
Notes	99

Acknowledgements and Translator's Note

I would like to thank Ms. Jennifer Eagleton, Dr. Finn Millar, Ms. Carmen K. M. Yu and Ms. Shelby K. Y. Chan for their assistance in editing and copyediting. Special thanks are also extended to the editors of The Chinese University Press, for preparing the manuscript for publication.

The present script was translated from the Chinese version published by United Publishing Co., Ltd 聯合文學 in Taipei in 2001, which has some changes from the earlier 1993 version published by Cosmos Books Ltd. 天地圖書 in Hong Kong.

There are more than 70 named characters in the play. I have tried, wherever possible, to translate the names semantically so that they are meaningful to the English reader. Transliterations are used where the characters' names are established or their meanings are obscure or undecipherable.

Gilbert C. F. Fong

Introduction:
Purity of Origin

The return to the origin of purity and truth comes from modern man's renewed quest for and affirmation of his own value. The simplicity in modern literature was conceived in the strength and confidence of modern man (Gao 1983: 3).

> There are countless exegeses of *The Classic of Mountains and Seas* [*Shanhaijing* 山海經]—they can be made into a homily on ethics and morals, a heroic myth or even a means of promoting nationalism and patriotism. Yet I hope to strip all these away and revert the myths to their primal and unadorned state, then link up all the bits and pieces into a play.... The process is somewhat like an archeologist trying to restore the hundreds of broken pieces of a Grecian urn into its original condition, ... (Gao 2006)

The insistence on getting back to the source has always been one of the central tenets of Gao Xingjian's thinking on art, literature and the theater. This belief in the purity of origin has exerted tremendous influences on his writings, paintings and theater. Frequently in Gao's career, he would revert to the fount, be it an original text, legend, theater or what he considers primordial human nature, as inspiration for his work or as a refuge from the encroachment of politics and commercialism in the modern world, a world that has been corrupted and deprived of purity and innocence.

It is thus not surprising that Gao turned to *The Classic of Mountains and Seas* as the inspiration for his ancient Chinese mythological saga, as the ancient text, with its crude and archaic language, has a kind of "unprocessed" feel to it. The book is a rich source of Chinese mythology, and it has fascinated Chinese readers for more than two millennia with its depiction of natural and supernatural fauna and flora, strange beasts, animals and spiritual beings. It had been attributed to Yu the Great 大禹 (21st century B.C.), the ancient sage king famous for controlling the flood in mythical times, and his assistant Bo Yi 伯益. The Han dynasty historian Liu Xiu 劉秀 (formerly named Liu Xin 劉歆) wrote:

> Yu and Po Yi [Bo Yi] were put in charge of clearing out the birds and animals, naming the mountains and rivers, classifying plants and trees, and distinguishing water and land features.... Within, they distinguished the mountains of the five regions, and outside they discriminated the seas of the eight regions. They recorded the precious and unusual things of these strange places, the plants, trees, birds, animals, insects and rarely seen creatures of the waters and the land, where the good omens are concealed, along with the distant lands and different peoples beyond the four seas. (Liu 1985: 383)

Later studies found that the book had mixed origins, and that it was most likely put together by shamans, alchemists and local officials over a period of time. Scholars also disagree on the exact dating of the book, but it is generally believed that the chapters gradually came into being around the time of the Warring States Period in as early as the 4th century B.C. and was first compiled into a book in the Western Han dynasty by the father-and-son team of Liu Xiang 劉向 and Liu Xiu around 53 to 23 B.C. In its present form, *The Classic of Mountains and Seas* contains eighteen chapters (*juan* 卷) for a total of 31,000 characters, describing more than 100 foreign lands, 550 mountains, 300 waterways, 95 foreign lands and tribes, 130 kinds of medicinal herbs, 435 plants, 90 metals and minerals, and various mountain gods and forms of ritualistic sacrifices (Strassberg 2002: 3).

The study of Chinese mythology has never developed to the extent of that of Greek or Hindu mythologies. Some scholars, such as the famous writer Mao Dun 茅盾, have pointed their fingers at the historizing process in Chinese mythology, which resulted in a compulsion to transform gods and spirits into historical figures and record their stories in dynastic histories; others have adopted a Marxist viewpoint and argued that mythology was turned into a means of legitimization by members of the ruling class, i.e., by making the mythical heroes as the sage kings and princes of prehistoric times and claiming them as their ancestors, they were able to assert their ancient lineage and godly descent, thus legitimizing their rule (Yuan 1979: 3–9). There is no denying the pragmatic bent in Chinese culture, and thinkers and scholars, especially the Confucianists, tend to rationalize the irrational, and like Confucius himself, they eschew the supernatural. As Confucius said in *The Analects*, "The master did not discuss extraordinary things, feats of strength, disorder or spiritual beings" ("Shu Er": 45).

To Gao Xingjian, historizing mythology is almost sacrilegious, for it has contaminated the purity and managed to bury the "truth" of Chinese myths. In a personal interview he pointed out emphatically that in *Of Mountains and Seas* (*Shanhaijing zhuan* 山海經傳) he attempts to restore Chinese mythology to its original, unadulterated state, and to put in place a system which would organize the diverse materials scattered throughout the chapters of *The Classic of Mountains and Seas* and construct a "grand narrative" of the Chinese race. He added that he had read a large number of books and done meticulous research on the topic, and that unlike most Chinese scholars who only sit at their desks and speculate, he had actually conducted many field trips and visited the places mentioned in the book. His findings reinforced his conviction that the original myths had been corrupted by an unrelenting didacticism, as many of the stories had been turned into cautionary tales and heroic legends to spur people onto nationalistic thinking. With his play, he claims to have made a significant contribution to Chinese cultural history in purging ideology, politics and moralism from the corrupted myths and returning them to their originality (Gao 2004).

To reconstruct the Chinese mythological system in the course of a stage play is perhaps an overly ambitious goal. For our purposes, instead of treating the play as an illustration of Gao Xingjian's "grand narrative," we will make use of his system to analyze the structure of the play, which may be somewhat baffling at first glance. According to Gao Xingjian, "heaven" (*tian* 天) in the Chinese mythological world is made up of four domains, each having its own "emperor" as the supreme ruler. In the east there is the Able Emperor (Act I); in the south the Flame Emperor (Act II); in the west the Queen Mother of the West (Act II); and in the north the Yellow Emperor (Acts II and III). The play starts with the creation of human beings by Nü Wa (Act I) and ends with the founding of the Xia dynasty

(Act III), i.e., the beginning of the age of history of the Chinese nation and the end of the mythological era. The war between Chi You and the Yellow Emperor straddles the three acts and makes up the kernel of the play. (Gao Xingjian believes that the major action of most ancient myths is war, so war becomes an important structuration motif in *Of Mountains and Seas*.)

Another structuration device is Storyteller. As the narrator of the story of the gods, he is the thread that ties up loose ends and strings together the various episodes of the play. Description is thus added to the dramatic narration, facilitating the quick change of scenes, regulating the rhythm of the action and imparting to the play an epic quality of Homeric proportions. Gao Xingjian calls Storyteller *shuochang yiren* 說唱藝人, which literally means an artist who sings (*chang* 唱) and tells the story (*shuo* 說). A rhetorical narrator, he is always bent on philosophizing, commenting on the characters' actions, talking directly to the audience and reminding them that they are watching a performance on stage. The play actually bestows on Storyteller the role of the playwright's surrogate, assigning him the task of overseeing the proceedings and at the same time fashioning them to shape the play's structure.

The play is fragmented, device-baring and performance-conscious; in fact, with its self-reflexivity, it has all the makings of a Brechtian production. But unlike Brechtian theater, *Of Mountains and Seas* is not directed toward challenging the audience to an intellectual duel, nor is it aiming at the possibility of altering the audience's consciousness. Gao Xingjian has no pretensions to edification, be it moralistic or political, but this is not to say that the play is totally devoid of ideological implications. The indifference to a dogmatic orthodoxy and the move away from the center toward the margins may very well be indicative of the subversiveness in Gao Xingjian's art. There appeared to be a strong urge to redress the wrong of misreading *The Classic of Mountains and Seas* throughout the centuries, to "overturn the case of injustice" (*fan'an* 翻案) done to the ancient text so that its true colors could once again be revealed (Fong 2001: 103–6). Or as Quah Sy Ren says:

> … [T]he dramatic structure and characterization of these plays [*City of the Dead* and *Of Mountains and Seas*] as well as the playwright's explanatory notes illustrate that Gao's reflection on Chinese culture is a challenge to mainstream Confucian literati culture. To counter the hegemonic culture

of the Yellow River region, Gao upholds the marginalized cultures of the Yangtze region, which have an equally long history; to counter the canonized, dogmatized Confucian culture, Gao valorizes the cultures of secular Daoism and Chan Buddhism, which have strong folk and ritualistic characteristics; to counter the rigidified literati culture, Gao promotes an array of folk arts that are inextricably linked to people's everyday lives. (Quah 2004: 17)

But political or ideological subversion, according to Gao Xingjian, has to be clearly separated from art, and if we espouse confrontation and subversion as artistic strategies, they will take over art completely, and art will only become a mere footnote to political happenings (Gao 2007). With *Of Mountains and Seas* the subversiveness, though it may appear carnivalesque in the Bakhtinian sense, is not overtly ideological. It is often redirected to become satire and spills over into the realms of farce and comedy.

However, comedy cannot completely overwhelm the feeling of anti-establishment in the play. The more than seventy characters can roughly be categorized into two groups—the rulers and the ruled. The rulers are endowed with absolute power, which they readily and indiscriminately use to inflict suffering and injustice on the people; and the ruled, though most of them are gods with certain powers, are frequently cheated, exploited and usually given the short end of the stick. There are those in the latter group who challenge or rebel against authority; for example, Gong Gong who fights valiantly against the hegemonic Yellow Emperor; Headless the Reckless who keeps on fighting despite being decapitated; Gun who steals the Ever-growing Soil in Heaven to control the flood; the overreaching Big Talk who chases after the sun; and Yi the Archer who has offended the Able Emperor and the Sun Mother. Even Chi You, a traditional villain condemned for his presumptuousness, is portrayed rather positively in his effort to stop the overly ambitious Yellow Emperor from taking over the entire Heavenly kingdom. It is with these challengers and rebels that Gao Xingjian's sympathy undoubtedly lies. John Y. H. Hu has pointed out that *Of Mountains and Seas* portrays a world of totalitarianism, in which violence and chicanery reign supreme, and the ruling class and the Confucian sage kings, such as Shun (Able Emperor) and the Yellow Emperor, are portrayed negatively, condemned for their impotence, corruption, ruthlessness and deceit (Hu 1995: 27–32).

Gao Xingjian claims to have avoided moral judgment on the characters. To him, greed, ambition, jealousy, confrontation, love, lust and the thirst for power are all common to human nature, and they have been made into the personality traits of the gods in the play. These innate qualities, according to Gao, should not be regarded as good or evil, in the same way that human nature is not originally good or evil, so no matter they are the Yellow Emperor, Flame Emperor, Able Emperor or any other characters, they should not be evaluated according to any moral yardsticks. To use value judgment on them, in other words, to adopt a black-and-white view of the world, would have simplified the complexities of human nature and delimited the scope of Gao's examination of the Chinese collective consciousness, and more abhorrently, subjected the myths to extrinsic interpretations and thus further corruption by didacticism (Gao 2004).

The refusal to describe the particularities of the characters in favor of the commonalities of human nature results in the "flatness" in most of the characterizations in the play. Even Yi the Archer, who has been given a more multidimensional depiction, i.e., we know more about him than the other characters in terms of his ambition, love and desires, is nowhere near our understanding of psychological characterization. Sent by the Able Emperor to get rid of the beasts and monsters wreaking havocs in the world of men, Yi completes the mission dutifully and loyally, but in doing so he shoots down nine of the ten suns (the mischievous sons of Able Emperor), which have been scorching the earth and making people's lives unbearable. Besides suffering from the conflict of allegiances to the Emperor and the people, he is also torn between devotion to his wife and his desire for the seductive beauty of Fu Fei. Consequently the Able Emperor banishes him from Heaven for killing the Sons of Heaven, but he is also rejected by the ungrateful people on earth, despite the fact that his bravery has helped them to regain their peace and livelihood. Like modern man, he is oppressed by society and the power that be, and at the same time hounded by the masses. And as with our playwright when he was in China, Yi is under attack on every front. According to Gao Xingjian, Yi represents man's fate, and among the gods he is the closest to the consciousness of modern man (Gao 2004); through him, one can see a burgeoning self-consciousness and the trials and tribulations of being human.

Psychological realism is not at issue here; it has never been Gao

Xingjian's concern to portray his characters in the Stanislavskian fashion. To do so would have led to realistic excesses contrary to Gao's idea of the suppositionality of the theater (Quah 2004: 105–14). His instructions are for the performance to approximate the milieu of a temple fair and the actors to perform acrobatic tricks, like folk artists hawking their skills and wares on temple grounds.

> Our play is a return to the dramatic tradition of ancient China. I suggest that the performance should adopt the form of a variety show, borrowing elements from the styles of the roadside salesman, the medicine man, monkey shows, acrobatics, puppetry and shadow plays, and the candy man. The atmosphere may be likened to the hustle and bustle of a temple fair. (Gao 1989: 158)

To Gao, this represents uncorrupted theater, in the same way that he prefers the Storyteller in the play to deliver his narration in the incantatory style of the shamans in the southwestern part of China, the simple and "unaffected" legacy of primordial cultures. For the same reason, he calls for the unrefined simplicity of pre-Tang dynasty colors and patterns in set design.

It appears that in his plays Gao has gone out of his way to undermine realism, which in his opinion represents deception through a superficial portrayal of reality. He aims to dismantle all artificial and arbitrary constraints restricting freedom of expression in both form and content. The deployment of acrobatics and folk art forms and the shifts in point of view—using the second or third person in place of the first person "I"—certainly do not promote the convergence of theater and real life in his plays. His aspiration is for a higher plane of reality—the essence of theater, especially theater in its original form and spirit, and of the human psyche as experienced and perceived by the audience, not just something disguised and presented as reality.

In order to achieve his goal of a higher plane of reality, i.e., consciousness, Gao turns to blending the procedures of Western psychoanalysis and the "quiet observation" of Buddhism. This combination of the West and the East, which is found in most of his works, leads to the idea of a "third eye," a detaching and detached process of the subject but at the same time outside the subject itself for the purpose of self-scrutiny. He calls this self-forgetting process "observation" (*guanzhao* 觀照). In his psychological plays, the "observation" is "small" (*xiao guanzhao* 小觀照), in the sense that it is personal and confined to the self (the subject). With the epical plays, the "observation" is carried out on a larger scale. For instance, *Of Mountains and Seas* is an examination of collective consciousness, and the "observation" done on the extended self is "large" (*da guanzhao* 大觀照). The myths, folk songs and legends, all having collective authorship, together and diachronically form the basis of human communication; they are the beginning of individual self-consciousness. The Storyteller in the play, who is narrator, commentator and organizing principle all rolled into one, in fact plays the role of the "third eye" looking in from the outside to achieve a clear and unobstructed view of Chinese collective consciousness (Gao 2004).

The "third eye" is the means with which the artist transcends reality and achieves a clear observation, or *guanzhao*, free from subjectivity and value judgments based on ethics, morality, politics or good and evil. It is, however, not a mere recording mechanism, for it has to equip itself with conscientiousness in order to apprehend the predicament of being human. For Gao Xingjian, form is not entirely devoid of ideological implications, and the same is true of his search for new modes of expression. So his deployments of the epic in *Of Mountains and Seas*, the shamanistic chanting, the acrobatic tricks, etc., are not simply a restoration of traditional art forms. They are manifestations of a deep collective consciousness, and together with the myths, they make up what Gao calls a modern epic imbued with modern man's predicament. It is as if the Chinese race is a patient undergoing an examination of its inner psyche yet without employing the techniques of psychoanalysis, which our playwright eschews, especially in the theater. (This is where the "third eye" comes in.) Purity can thus be found in form and content, and in this presentation process, clarity is achieved as the artist is able to transcend himself and reality.

> And so mythologies have modern meanings, just as Greek tragedies of centuries ago are still able to stir men's most fundamental sentiments.... Human evolution is an endless process, and things like basic desires, sexual relationships and power struggles do not change with time. There might be changes in form, but the basic relationships are still there. This is exactly where my search took place. (Gao 2006)

In an article entitled "The Faith in Truth" (Gao 2001: 123–27), Gao Xingjian points out that many artists have advocated "Truth is Beauty," but the relationship between "truth" and "beauty" may not be absolute or necessary, even though a connection between art and reality clearly exists. How does art then describe reality? There are various ways: expression (*biaoxian* 表現), representation (*zaixian* 再現), or presentation (*chengxian* 呈現), and any one of them is possible and viable as an artistic method to describe the world we live in. Despite the apparent lack of preference, Gao clearly eschews realistic representation and favors presentation, i.e., the direct manifestation of reality.

In the case of *Of Mountains and Seas*, the compulsion to go back to the original source, i.e., to purge the myths of their impurities, is paramount. In order to have an unmediated picture of human nature in its rawness and multifariousness, and to delineate the collective consciousness of the Chinese people in its initial purity, Gao has decided to go back to the original classical texts, ignoring the histories, didactic exegeses and interpretations by scholars. The characters in the plays, as he says, are as they are described in the original myths (Gao 2004). The purpose is to "present" an uncorrupted view before the arrival of morality. But there is a twist—his presentation is in fact a second-tier presentation or representation, i.e., one that attempts to cleanse the corruption by previous presentation(s). This feeling of self-righteousness is typical in Gao Xingjian's work.

The artistic world of Gao Xingjian consists mainly of three aspects: the artist, the world (reality), and truth.

> To the artist, truth is closely bound up with his sincerity toward art. His goal is the unity of aesthetics and ethics, and he would rather achieve his faith in truth through concrete feelings. This is also the more or less secure footing from which he, as a normal individual, fights against this world of madness. On the part of the artist, the return to individual aesthetic feelings is also the means of protecting art and engaging in self-salvation. As for the polemics on truth, it should be left to the philosophers …
>
> The artist should equip himself with the feelings for reality, and he should also try to express these feelings. The process has to be founded upon his faith in truth, which to the artist is tantamount to sincerity. Being sincere to his own work is the special kind of morality for an artist. (Gao 2001: 125–27)

The world, or reality, has taken on the role of the artist's adversary; it encroaches upon the individual and is the source of corruption which obscures truth. The antipathy toward the world notwithstanding, it is the hurdle the artist must overcome; in any case it is the object of the artist's feelings and thus a necessity on the path toward truth. In regarding the world, the artist has to be "sincere" (*zhencheng* 真誠), i.e., true to his feelings, and to Gao Xingjian this is an ethical issue. As in classical Chinese art and literature, sincerity is the code to which the artist has to subscribe; this is where and how the expressive function of art is tied in with the artist's individuality. The artistic process is once again focused on art and the artist—to protect the integrity of art and to engage in the artist's self-salvation. Meanwhile, the artist has to rise above his self, which is entrenched in worldliness, in order to reach for a clear and unobstructed view of the world. Gao Xingjian calls this transcendental process "quiet observation," and in writing it becomes "cold literature," a highly personal endeavor unrelated to other people, politics, social intervention or any form of utilitarian function (Fong 2005: viii).

> The world has absolutely no order. Only when one transcends oneself and engages in "quiet observation" can one achieve clarity in the process. (Gao 1992: 288)

Evidently, the conflict in writing *Of Mountains and Seas* is between artifice and naturalness; between civilization's conception of human nature (the morality of good and evil) and its prehistoric (mythical) amorality; and between didacticism and truth. The goal of "quiet observation"—the artistic process—is "clarity," unmediated, uncorrupted, unobstructed, pure and simple. Gao Xingjian constantly pursues the first and the original in art, and that is the reason why he regards writing as the purification process of both the matter and the self.

References

Fong, Gilbert C. F. 方梓勳 (2001). "Cong fan'an dao lingyizhong xiju: Tan *Shanhaijing zhuan*" 從翻案到另一種戲劇：談《山海經傳》 [From overturning the case to another kind of drama: On *Of Mountains and Seas*]. *UNITAS A Literary Monthly Journal* 聯合文學, February 2001: 103–6.

—— (2005). "Freedom and Marginality: The Life and Art of Gao Xingjian". In Gao

Xingjian, *Cold Literature*, edited and translated by Gilbert C. F. Fong and Mabel Lee. Hong Kong: The Chinese University Press.

Gao, Xingjian 高行健 (1983). "Zhipu yu chunjie" 質樸與純潔 [Simplicity and purity]. *Wenxue bao* 文學報 [Literature press] (Shanghai), No. 112, May 19, 1983: 3.

—— (1989). *Shanhaijing zhuan* 山海經傳 [Of Mountains and Seas]. Taipei: Unitas Publishing Co., Ltd. 聯合文學.

—— (1992). "Tan wode hua" 談我的畫 [On my paintings]. In *Meiyou zhuyi* 沒有主義 [Without isms]. Hong Kong: Cosmos Books Limited 天地圖書有限公司.

—— (2001). "Dui zhenshi de xinnian" 對真實的信念 [The faith in truth]. In *Wenxue de liyou* 文學的理由 [The case for literature]. Hong Kong: Ming Pao Publications Limited 明報出版社有限公司.

—— (2004). Interview by the writer. Paris, July 28, 2004.

—— (2006). Interview by the writer. Paris, June 21, 2006.

—— (2007). "Yishujia de meixue" 藝術家的美學 [The artist's aesthetics]. Manuscript.

Hu, John Y. H. 胡耀恆 (1995). *Bainian gengyun de fengshou* 百年耕耘的豐收 [Bumper harvest of a hundred years of cultivation]. Taipei: Dijiao chubanshe 帝教出版社.

Liu, Hsiu (1985). "Preface (Memorial to the Throne)". In *Shan Hai Ching Legendary Geography and Wonders of Ancient China*, translated by Hsiao-Chieh Cheng, Hui-Chen Pai Cheng and Kenneth Lawrence Thern. Taipei: The Committee for Compilation and Examination of the Series of Chinese Classics, National Institute for Compilation and Translation.

Quah, Sy Ren (2004). *Gao Xingjian and Transcultural Chinese Theater.* Honolulu: University of Hawai'i Press.

"Shu Er" 述而 (1968). In *Lunyu: Sishu jizhu* 論語：四書集註 [Confucian analects: Collected commentaries on *The Four Books*]. Hong Kong: Taiping shuju 太平書局.

Strassberg, Richard E., ed. and trans. (2002). *A Chinese Bestiary: Strange Creatures from the Guideways through Mountains and Seas.* Berkeley: University of California Press.

Yuan, Ke 袁珂 (1979). "Qianyan" 前言 [Preface]. In *Gu shenhua xuanshi* 古神話選釋 [Exegeses of selected ancient myths]. Beijing: Renmin wenxue chubanshe 人民文學出版社.

List of Illustrations

1. Nü Wa 女媧
2. Five-Colored Bird 五采鳥
3. Yi the Archer (Hou Yi 后羿)
4. Tree God (Gou Mang 句芒)
5. Ten Women Shamans 十巫
6. Chi You 蚩尤
7. Queen Mother of the West (Xi Wang Mu 西王母)
8. Yu Hao 禺虢
9. Winged Dragon (Ying Long 應龍)
10. Thunder Beast (Lei Shou 雷獸)
11. Giant Ox (Kui Niu 夔牛)
12. Big Talk (Kua Fu 夸父)
13. Headless the Reckless (Xing Tian 刑天)
14. Long-Life Hemp (Shou Ma 壽麻)
15. Fire God (Zhu Rong 祝融)
16. Autumn God (Ru Shou 蓐收)
17. Aide Willow (Xiang Liu 相柳)

1. Nü Wa

2. Five-Colored Bird

3. Yi the Archer

4. Tree God

5. Ten Women Shamans

6. Chi You

7. Queen Mother of the West

8. Yu Hao

9. Winged Dragon

10. Thunder Beast

11. Giant Ox

12. Big Talk

13. Headless the Reckless

14. Long-Life Hemp

15. Fire God

16. Autumn God

17. Aide Willow

Of Mountains and Seas

Cast of Characters

(*In order of their appearance*):

Storyteller 說唱藝人

Nü Wa 女媧

Ten Humans 十神人

Fu Xi 伏羲

Able Emperor (Di Jun 帝俊)

Five-Colored Bird 五采鳥

Sun Mother (Xi He 羲和)

Moon Mother (Chang Yi 常儀)

Ten Suns 十金烏

People 百姓

Monsters: Ya Yu 猰貐, Chiseled Teeth 鑿齒, Nine-Headed Monster 九嬰, Big Wind Peacock 大風, Big Pig 封豨 and Long Snake 修蛇

Woman Clown 女丑

Yi the Archer (Hou Yi 后羿)

Chang E 嫦娥

Tree God (Gou Mang 句芒)

Flame Emperor (Yan Di 炎帝)

Dolly (Nü Wa 女娃)

Ten Women Shamans 十巫: Shaman Xian 巫咸, Shaman Ji 巫即, Shaman Fen 巫盼, Shaman Peng 巫彭, Shaman Gu 巫姑, Shaman Zhen 巫真, Shaman Li 巫禮, Shaman Di 巫抵, Shaman Xie 巫謝, Shaman Luo 巫羅

Chi You 蚩尤

Fu Fei 宓妃

River Lord (He Bo 河伯)

Yellow Emperor (Huang Di 黃帝)

Black Bear 熊, Brown Bear 羆, Tiger 虎, Leopard 豹

Wind Master and Rain Chief 風師、雨伯

Queen Mother of the West (Xi Wang Mu 西王母)

Four Ghosts: Chi 魑, Mei 魅, Wang 魍, Liang 魉

Yu Hao 禹虢

Yu Jing 禹京

Winged Dragon (Ying Long 應龍)

Aridity (Ba 魃)

Thunder Beast (Lei Shou 雷獸)

Giant Ox (Kui Niu 夔牛)

Big Talk (Kua Fu 夸父)

Headless the Reckless (Xing Tian 刑天)

Long-Life Hemp (Shou Ma 壽麻)

Fire God (Zhu Rong 祝融)

Shao Hao 少昊

Autumn God (Ru Shou 蓐收)

Zhuan Xu 顓頊

Earth God (Hou Tu 后土)

The Brothers Chong and Li 重、黎兩兄弟

Gong Gong 共工

Gun 鯀

Chi Owl 鴟

Tortoise 龜

Shen Tu 神荼

Yu Lei 鬱壘

Wu the Knife (Wu Dao 吳刀)

Yu 禹

Aide Willow (Xiang Liu 相柳)

Pretty Maid (Nü Jiao 女嬌)

The Gods 眾神

Windshield (Fang Feng Shi 防風氏)

Hiker (Shu Hai 豎亥)

An actor or actress can play several of the following characters when they appear at different times:

Ten Humans, Ten Suns, People, The Gods, Nü Wa, Fu Xi, Moon Mother, Chiseled Teeth, Nine-Headed Monster, Big Wind Peacock, Ya Yu, Long Snake, Big Pig, Tree God, River Lord, Black Bear, Brown Bear, Tiger, Leopard, Wind Master, Rain Chief, Chi, Mei, Wang, Liang, Watchman, Long-Life Hemp, Fire God, Shao Hao, Earth God, Gong Gong, Chi Owl, Tortoise, Wu the Knife, Aide Willow, Pretty Maid, Windshield, and Hiker.

Act I

[Enter STORYTELLER *carrying a broken gong. He is bald-headed, wearing cloth shoes and a long robe with long, wide sleeves.*

STORYTELLER Ladies and gentlemen, welcome to our show. My goodness, a full house. Anyone knows what's on tonight? It's called *Of Mountains and Seas*, uncut and unabridged! (*Beats the gong once.*)

The Classic of Mountains and Seas is a very ancient book. Nobody knows when it was written or who wrote it. Anyway, it's very, very old. It tells of impossible but weird and wonderful things, like many-headed animals, headless creatures with human bodies and birds with three feet. There are also one-legged cows, snakes with human faces, foxes with nine tails and whatnot. They all look human, but they're not. They're all mighty talented, though a little lacking in love and morality.

Ladies and gentlemen, please do give them your kind indulgence. They're strange, but you'll get used to them. (*Beats the gong again.*)

Enough of this idle talk. Let's return to the good old book *The Classic of Mountains and Seas*, which chronicles the formation of the sun and the moon, the making of humans from a goddess' bowels, how the gods kick up a row in Heaven, and how the Sons of Heaven fight among themselves on earth. They say it's always difficult to start something, but all good shows have got to have a good beginning, haven't they? (*Beats the gong, now broken, continuously. Exit.*)

[*Suddenly different kinds of sounds in the universe break out all at once. There are flashing earth lights and polar lights, just as in a big earthquake, an erupting volcano or crashing meteors. Amidst this great chaos, the naked Nü Wa is seen sitting unfazed, her disheveled long hair flowing down her shoulders. Rain is pouring and torrents come gushing down the mountain, gradually turning into gurgling water in a river. The river then turns into a small stream and finally becomes bubbling water droplets. Then all is dead silence. Nü Wa slowly lifts her head, murmuring.*

Enter STORYTELLER, *lifting up the long robe he is wearing and carrying a muffled drum on his back.*

STORYTELLER (*Beats the drum once.*) Ladies and gentlemen, please take a look at our ancestress in this vast wilderness. They call her Nü Wa. She's a goddess, so of course she's no ordinary woman. She's very dirty, yet also extremely pretty; she has no shame, yet she's prim and proper. Nobody knows what she's saying or what she's singing. The gods have their own language. You and I are mere mortals—how could we ever understand?

Look at this Nü Wa. She is as wild as she is wanton, and as tender as she is melancholy. She sings to amuse herself, heedless of the loneliness in this place between Heaven and earth. A happy-go-lucky goddess she is indeed.

[*Nü Wa sings and sways from side to side, her hands keep kneading something.*

STORYTELLER You know, she has the face of a human but the body of a snake. And she can perform seventy different transformations, all in one day! (*Beats the drum twice.*)

It has come to pass that the four corners of the earth are no more; the nine prefectures have cracked open. The sky offers no shelter; the earth cannot hold. Water gushes in endless torrents; raging flames refuse to die down. Wild beasts prowl and devour people and vultures swoop down from the sky to seize the young; even the elderly can't escape from their pitiless claws. Good Nü Wa, (*Beats drum and sings in a high-pitched voice.*) she melts stones of five colors to patch the hole in the sky; she cuts off the four legs of a giant turtle and uses them to prop up the four corners of the earth; she kills the black dragon to save the people of the nine prefectures; she burns river reeds and piles up the ashes to stop the flood.

[*Nü Wa lies supine, her hands pointing toward the sky. Wailing loudly she tosses and turns as if drunk or mad. The* Ten Humans, *who have been sprawling under her feet, crawl their way up inch by inch.*

STORYTELLER (*Moves back and observes.*) Look at the Ten Humans who are blocking the road in this vast wilderness. I bet they were all made from just one section of Nü Wa's bowels!

[*The* Humans, *forming a circle around Nü Wa, arch their backs and dance, their feet stamping the ground.*

STORYTELLER Believe it or not, many years from now people will say that when Nü Wa created human beings, she actually used clay. Still others say that it was not her bowels but a piece of string—as soon as she gave the string a jerk, hosts of men and women appeared all over the place.

[*Nü Wa throws away a piece of string and stretches lazily.*

The HUMANS, sticking out their chests and raising their heads, wave their hands and dance with their feet.

STORYTELLER   She gives them each a mouth, a face, two hands and two feet. They're all different, so that others can tell them apart. And without exception, all are given a tongue.

[*All crane their necks and stick out their tongues.*

STORYTELLER   Now that they've got tongues, they can eat and drink, they can learn to taste things, and they can all learn to talk.

[*All make continuous babbling sounds.*

STORYTELLER   Now they can express their emotions, they can tell people they love them, but then they can also tell people off, squabble among themselves, swear, curse and lie. Black becomes white, right becomes wrong, things turn topsy-turvy and the world becomes a noisy place, all for one reason—the mouth! (*Takes out a pair of hardwood plaques and claps them. Then he stops abruptly.*)

[*Suddenly all freeze.*

STORYTELLER   That's right. Everybody is given a pair of eyes, which can set apart light from darkness, distinguish colors, see faraway things, send out love signals and give others angry looks. Of course they can also express shock, beg for sympathy, shed tears and break into a smile—it doesn't matter if they're for real or not.

[*Nü WA, seeing the performance put on by all, claps her hands and bursts out laughing.*

STORYTELLER   In their chests there is also a pulsating heart made of flesh and blood. It can feel pain, understand ideas, repent of mistakes and be grateful or jealous. In the end, all hearts must fail; otherwise, the nonstop breeding of humans would result in overpopulation, precipitating a disaster that would perhaps deprive the gods of their heavenly abodes. People die either of the plague or of famine. As for killing each other, that's not part of the Creator's design.

[*All collapse one by one. The ground is strewn with dead bodies. Intermittent drumbeat, which soon stops altogether.*]

STORYTELLER　There is another story of how Nü Wa created human beings. (*Taps the drum lightly.*) It is said that she copulated with Fu Xi, also one of the forefathers, with a human head and a snake's body, to breed a great multitude of descendants. Generations afterward, they became known as the "Children of the Dragon"! (*Exit silently.*)

[*Nü Wa and Fu Xi, both with a human face and the body of a snake, stand up and embrace each other. Their figures gradually disappear.*

Enter STORYTELLER. *He has on a long gown with a cloth belt tied at the waist. He is wearing a wooden mask with a big mouth slanting to one side. There is a pair of cymbals hanging around his neck.*]

STORYTELLER　(*Crashes the cymbals together once.*) After the story of Creation, it's time to tell you about the emperors in Heaven. Ladies and gentlemen, *The Classic of Mountains and Seas* is not like the Bible of the West. Here, Heaven is vast and boundless. How can such a big Heaven be monopolized by one master? The land of China is divided into nine big provinces; as for the sky, it has no limits to start with. East, West, North, South and the Middle, each has its own emperor. There's got to be some division of labor. All the emperors in Heaven, and there are many of them, are supreme and the highest—how can they put up with one another and live in peace? Well, we storytellers have only one thing going for us—we know how to shoot off our mouths. So let me first introduce to you Jun, the Able Emperor, Heavenly Emperor of the East. (*Bangs the cymbals together continuously.*)

[*Enter the* ABLE EMPEROR, *one-legged and hopping up and down on a bamboo stick. He has the head of a bird and the body of a monkey. His face is black, and on his head are two horns.*

Enter FIVE-COLORED BIRD *after the* ABLE EMPEROR. *It looks like a phoenix, flapping its wings as it jigs about.*

Exit STORYTELLER *after bowing to the* ABLE EMPEROR.

ABLE EMPEROR My friend.

FIVE-COLORED BIRD Ji-ji.

ABLE EMPEROR Your dancing isn't too bad, but your singing is terrible.

FIVE-COLORED BIRD Your Majesty, a truly beautiful bird doesn't have to sing to show off its charms, only ugly birds need to do that.

ABLE EMPEROR Sounds reasonable.

FIVE-COLORED BIRD Besides, if there really is such a bird, as beautiful as it is good at singing, then why does Your Majesty have to keep so many birds?

ABLE EMPEROR Good point.

FIVE-COLORED BIRD Your Majesty has such a huge imperial court. Wouldn't you feel lonely if there weren't hundreds of birds singing and dancing for you day and night?

ABLE EMPEROR I would, that's true. Now go and see what my two wives are up to.

FIVE-COLORED BIRD	(*Cranes its neck and spreads its wings to look.*) Your wife the Sun Mother is now in Sunrise Valley. She's bathing your ten newborn sons in the bubbling hot Sweet Pool.
ABLE EMPEROR	(*Laughs.*) Those little darlings …
FIVE-COLORED BIRD	They all dazzle the eye, every single one of them. So lovely, so lively.
ABLE EMPEROR	They're indeed perfect.
FIVE-COLORED BIRD	Your Majesty's pride and joy!
ABLE EMPEROR	Now try to find my other wife, Moon Mother Chang Yi. What's she been doing all day?
FIVE-COLORED BIRD	Your good wife the Moon Mother is always so graceful, so quiet and demure—
ABLE EMPEROR	She's always unwell.
FIVE-COLORED BIRD	That's only because she has borne you twelve daughters. I see her now, she's dressing the girls and combing their hair one by one.
ABLE EMPEROR	No matter how you dress them up, you can't hide their inborn deficiencies. (*Very troubled.*) Get them here. I've got something to tell them.
FIVE-COLORED BIRD	(*Loudly.*) Your Majesties Empress Sun Mother and Empress Moon Mother, His Majesty requests your company!
	[*The* ABLE EMPEROR *sits high up on the platform.* FIVE-COLORED BIRD *spreads its wings to welcome the two empresses. Enter* SUN MOTHER. *She is elegant and poised, and is wearing a tall crown, on which are crouched six dragons.*
SUN MOTHER	Your Majesty, you'd better go and take a look at your darling sons! Each one is naughtier than the other, as

	if they're all trying to outdo each other with their mischief!
ABLE EMPEROR	My dear wife, they're your sons too. You know very well that you gave birth to the ten of them, all in one go!
SUN MOTHER	If you think ten is not enough—
ABLE EMPEROR	Oh no, please, no more. My good wife, my side of Heaven may be big, but there's only room for one sun. As long as it goes around our land from the East to the West every day, the people will know when to start working and when to take a rest, and they'll not become slothful. So one is enough! Enough!
SUN MOTHER	Your Majesty, are you getting tired of me?
ABLE EMPEROR	What're you saying, my dear? I love you, in more ways than one. Just don't give me any more sons.
SUN MOTHER	Good or bad, they're yours, your Sons of Heaven. Tell me, who else but you can give birth to suns? Never mind the number, they're all your children. You've got to take them as they come!
ABLE EMPEROR	Of course, but they really are a big problem. (*To* FIVE-COLORED BIRD.) Got any bright ideas?
FIVE-COLORED BIRD	Ji-ji. (*Tilting its head to one side.*) The Sons of Heaven are still young. If they work shifts, they'll be all right, and they probably won't tire themselves out so easily.
ABLE EMPEROR	That's not a bad idea.
SUN MOTHER	The children are still babies. How could you ask them to take on such strenuous work?
ABLE EMPEROR	When they're off duty, that is, when they've finished doing their rounds, they can don their black-feather coats, put their feet up and relax on top of the tall Fu Sang tree like the birds.

Sun Mother	But they're not birds! They're the Sons of Heaven, they've got to have somewhere to play!
Able Emperor	Then let them play all they want in Sweet Pool. This Celestial Court doesn't allow boisterous behavior.
Sun Mother	Your Majesty, may I go now?
Able Emperor	My dear, as long as you take good care of our children, you can come here any time. My friend here wants to summon birds of every shape and color to assemble at the Celestial Court. We can listen to them sing.

[Sun Mother *pays no attention. Exit.*

Able Emperor	Are all women on earth as good-tempered as the goddesses in Heaven?
Five-Colored Bird	Ji-ji.

[Enter Moon Mother, *wearing a laurel wreath on her head. She is fair and graceful.*

Moon Mother	Your Majesty, your daughters will soon have finished dressing themselves. They're awaiting your summons.
Able Emperor	They should make themselves beautiful. Let them take their time. I sent for you because I wanted to talk to you about them. As you can see, I have to take care of everything in Heaven as well as on earth, no matter how big or small it is. There has been nobody to help me. Now that I have so many sons and daughters, don't you think I should get some help from them so that I can have some time to myself?
Five-Colored Bird	Ji-ji.
Able Emperor	What're we going to do with our twelve daughters? We can't tell them to go on duty in the sky all at once and let the people find out what flaws they have. You know it as well as I do, people have sharp tongues

	and they wouldn't hesitate to use them to cause trouble. And we can't ask the one perfect daughter to go on duty all the time either. How could we, as parents, bear to see her tiring herself out night after night? They're our children, every one of them. Favoritism is out of the question. We have to find a way—in work and in play they have to be treated as equals. Otherwise, people will start talking and they'll become suspicious and jealous of one another.
MOON MOTHER	Whatever you say; your daughters wouldn't dare contradict you.
ABLE EMPEROR	Tell me, my friend, have you any good ideas?
FIVE-COLORED BIRD	I'm not sure if I should say this. I think that Your Majesty is overstraining yourself for the sake of the people.
ABLE EMPEROR	Why do you say that?
FIVE-COLORED BIRD	You tell your Sons of Heaven to tour the earth during the day. Why? Because then there'll be bumper crops all over the land, and the people will lead happy and peaceful lives. You also tell your Daughters of Heaven to hold up the heavenly lanterns at night, so that the people can make merry and enjoy themselves. But they still cause trouble and fight. If they keep on doing this night after night, how will they have any strength left to farm their land during the day? Don't you agree, Your Majesty?
ABLE EMPEROR	You really are a clever bird. What a shame! On earth there are too many smart people, but in the sky clever birds are few and far between. Well then, we'll ask the girls to work shifts. If they're indisposed, they can take a day off. We can't do anything about it. Women have more troubles than men. My dear wife, that's my decision. Do as I've told you. Now off you go.

[*Exit* Moon Mother.]

ABLE EMPEROR I should go to the bamboo grove to hear the birds sing.
A Heavenly Emperor is entitled to have a hobby too.
(*Exit with* Five-Colored Bird.)

[*Enter* Storyteller *beating the cymbals continuously.*

The Ten Suns, *three-footed, wearing gold headgear and draped with black-feather coats, jump up to the Fu Sang tree one by one.*

TEN SUNS (*Sing.*) The Heavenly Emperor is our father,
The Sun Goddess our mother.
We're born to be happy,
Make merry, there's nothing we do better.

What is sorrow? We don't know,
He who feels sad is a clown.
The Celestial Court, it's so huge,
We shouldn't just jump up and down.

There's our father's dragon chariot,
Dozing is Grey Dragon, the charioteer.
Quick! Wake up, you lazybones,
Take us to play far and near!
(*They jump off the tree one by one, screaming.*)

All right you, drive the chariot! Drive!
(*Exeunt running.*)

[*The dragon chariot roars across the Celestial Court. Enter* People, *running around in confusion.*

PEOPLE One, two, three, four, five, six, seven, eight, nine,
Goodness gracious! Ten suns! They're all out at once!
I bet Heaven's drunk. My goodness!
My goodness! Heaven's a mess!
Rice sprouts all dried up,
Big cracks in the fields everywhere.

Look at the tortoises and turtles. Their feet are pointing at the sky,
There are only stones in the rivers.
Come quick! Hide in the forest!
A forest fire is raging.
My! The animals have all come out of hiding!
(*Exeunt scurrying.*)

[*Enter monsters* YA YU, CHISELED TEETH, NINE-HEADED MONSTER, BIG WIND PEACOCK, BIG PIG *and* LONG SNAKE *dashing about and making threatening gestures. Then exeunt shrieking and howling.*

Enter the TEN SUNS *riding on the dragon chariot and brandishing their feather coats.*

TEN SUNS (*Sing.*) We're all noble Sons of Heaven,
Unlike the pathetic spawn of common folk.
Live, and live happily,
Play, and play hard.
Yee-ha! Away! Drive on! Ha-ha—Ha-ha! (*Exeunt driving the dragon chariot.*)

[*Enter* PEOPLE. *Some are carrying a* qing *(stone percussion instrument) or a* gui *(jade tablet). Others are holding a white dog, a white rooster or sheaves of rice in their hands. They are crowding around* WOMAN CLOWN *and pushing her along.*

WOMAN CLOWN *is dressed in green. Her hair is disheveled and her face is grimy. She is carrying a huge crab on her back.*

PEOPLE We've put food in your mouth,
And a roof over your head.
We've paid homage to you,
As if you were a god.
We've provided for you this long,
Disaster is upon us.
Show us your power now!

Woman Clown	White refined rice,
	White-feathered rooster,
	On the altar,
	For the gods.
	Sprinkle and splash,
	White dog's hot blood.
	Strike the *qing* stone,
	Sound the jade tablet!
	Seniors and elders,
	Follow this shaman.
	We kowtow and we kneel,
	We pray to Heaven above!
People	(*Kneel and pray.*) Gods on high, show us mercy,
	Listen to our plea, give us sweet rain!
Woman Clown	(*She performs her magical tricks as she drags the big crab around the altar, dancing and jumping up and down.*)
	Big crab, big crab, off you go, to the East Sea!
	Rain Chief and Wind Master, please come,
	And Thunder God too;
	And Fu Xi, your godly powers reign far and wide,
	Even the Tree God, who rides on the wind and two dragons,
	Has to listen to your orders!
	Big crab, big crab, take me for a ride!
	(*She is astounded to find that the big crab is dead.*)
	[*A loud roar in the sky. The dragon chariot speeds by. It grows hotter.*
Ten Suns	(*Sing.*) Our lives came from ma and pa,
	Our pleasures we find for ourselves.
	We're free and easy,
	We go anywhere we please.
Woman Clown	(*Covers her face with her clothing. Dodges left and right and tries to hide.*)
	Please spare my life—

People (*Extremely angry.*)
You eat well and live well,
We've provided for you for nothing. How dare you deceive us?
You said you could summon the wind and the rain, didn't you?
Where are your magical powers now? Explain yourself!
Don't let her fool us with her talk of gods and spirits, Burn this witch at the stake! Burn her now!
Offer her as a sacrifice to Heaven! Make her pay for her sins!
This wicked bitch has got to be punished by Heaven!

[Woman Clown *is burned to death by the hot suns.* People *are scared.*

Enter Ya Yu, Chiseled Teeth, Nine-Headed Monster, Big Wind Peacock, Big Pig *and* Long Snake. People *scatter in all directions, pursued by the monsters.*

Enter Able Emperor *in a hurry with* Five-Colored Bird.

Able Emperor (*Strikes the dragon-head scepter on the ground three times.*) Outrageous! Where are the celestial guards?

[*Enter* Yi the Archer *in a hurry.*

Yi Your servant Yi at your service.

Able Emperor It's pandemonium on earth. The cries and screams are reaching up to the sky and shaking Heaven. What's the matter with you? Are you deaf and blind?

Yi Your Majesty, Ya Yu, Chiseled Teeth, Nine-Headed Dragon, Big Wind Peacock, Big Pig and Long Snake are stirring up trouble. The people have deserted their lands and they're suffering immensely. How could I not know anything about it?

ABLE EMPEROR	If you were aware of the problem, why haven't you tried to overcome the monsters? Aren't you being remiss in carrying out your duties?
YI	I wouldn't dare act rashly without Your Majesty's order.
ABLE EMPEROR	(*To FIVE-COLORED BIRD.*) Bring my red bow and white arrows and give them to him. Now go and make the earth a peaceful place to live again!
YI	(*Accepts the bow and arrows.*) Yes, Your Majesty. Thank you, Your Majesty.
ABLE EMPEROR	Anyone who dares to cause trouble, kill them! Ask questions later.
YI	I'm afraid—
ABLE EMPEROR	The red bow and white arrows in your possession are tokens of empowerment, need I say more?

[*Enter SUN MOTHER. Exit YI.*]

ABLE EMPEROR	You've arrived just in time. As the human world needs order, the Celestial Court also requires rules. I hope you didn't turn a blind eye to my orders?
SUN MOTHER	You told the children to take turns going on an inspection tour every day, from the Sun and Moon Mountain in the East Sea to Sunset Mountain on West Point, didn't you?
ABLE EMPEROR	But now they're having a ball, on the rampage, riding my dragon chariot around Heaven!
SUN MOTHER	You have to remember that they've only just been born. You yourself ask these babies to take on such a tiring official duty. And you take it easy yourself, spending all day listening to the birds sing. I don't appreciate these fawning feathered friends who know only how to wag their glib tongues.

[*Exit* Five-Colored Bird *in a hurry, closing its wings and tiptoeing.*]

Able Emperor: Babies indeed! They've turned the world upside down. Even I can't get a moment's peace!

Sun Mother: Then you shouldn't have had sons and I shouldn't have been a mother.

Able Emperor: Take a look … (*Looks back and finds* Five-Colored Bird *gone.*) Just some inconsequential birds. Don't get all worked up on their account. If I were fooling around with the goddesses all day—

Sun Mother: Don't mention them in my presence!

Able Emperor: Look at you, you're all worked up. I'm not just someone's husband, my dear wife. I'm also a Heavenly God.

Sun Mother: Then you tell Chang E to go with Yi. They should both go down to earth together. As a wife, she should follow wherever her husband goes, shouldn't she?

Able Emperor: They all say it's tough being a man, but it's even tougher being a Heavenly God. (*Exit with* Sun Mother.)

[*Enter* Yi *carrying the red bow and the white arrows. He plays with the metal arrowheads and then bends back the bow.*

Yi: (*Happy with himself.*) What a bow and what arrows! Watch out, all you monsters and troublemakers!

[*Enter* Chang E *in a hurry, her long gown flowing.*

Chang E: The Heavenly Goddess wanted me to accompany you down to earth. She said that it was the Heavenly God's wish.

Yi: If you don't go with me, I'll probably stay behind in the Kingdom of Women with its legion of beautiful

	girls. I won't even want to come back to the Celestial Court. You're not afraid?
CHANG E	It's your problem if you covet the transient beauty on earth and betray your love for me so easily. I won't be alone for long, you know, there are so many gods in Heaven to choose from.
YI	Just kidding. Forget what I said.
CHANG E	I don't want to leave you either. We're newlyweds, remember?
YI	Then you should come down to earth with me. I want to let all the gods know that Yi can be more than a yawning doorman at Heaven's Gate. Look, your husband's magic powers are limitless!
CHANG E	Whatever happens on earth is not my concern. I'm just worried … Yi, I don't know why I'm feeling so fidgety. I have this premonition—
YI	Nonsense! What's there to be afraid of when you're with me? My dear, come with me to conquer the world! (*Exit, taking* CHANG E *with him.*)

[*Earth. The noise is ear-splitting. Enter* YA YU, CHISELED TEETH, NINE-HEADED MONSTER, BIG WIND PEACOCK, BIG PIG *and* LONG SNAKE *chasing after* PEOPLE. *Enter* YI *from the opposite direction, with* CHANG E *following.*

YI — The invincible Yi is here! Watch out, all you stupid animals! Haven't you heard of Yi the Archer? If he aims for the throat, he'll not get the chin, and if he points at the eyeball, he won't touch one hair on the eyebrow. The hawks and falcons in the sky, and the flood dragons in the water, they've all had a taste of Yi's arrows. His arrows are no vegetarians—once he shoots them off, they've got to hit meat. And you're looking right at him! You hear me? You stupid sons of bitches!

[YA YU *howls and leaps forward. He falls immediately after being shot with an arrow.* CHISELED TEETH *makes threatening gestures with his teeth and fangs, trying to attack* YI *from behind.* YI *turns and sends the monster flying with an arrow. The monsters all recoil in horror. Seeing* YI *bending his bow, they scurry away, but are killed one by one. Enter* PEOPLE *one after another.*

PEOPLE Aren't you the mighty Yi the Archer from Heaven? Please allow us to pay you our respects by kneeling before you. We're poor and lowly people, we don't know how to show our gratitude in a proper manner.

YI I'm no more than an errand runner of the Heavenly God himself, who has sent me down here to rid the earth of harm and disaster. Get up quickly, all of you. There's no need to worship me like that.

PEOPLE The Heavenly God is too far away from us,
No matter how we pray our words don't reach the edge of Heaven.
The lord on high must be really tired of us,
That's why he's punished us in this way.
We should be thankful that you've been sent from Heaven above.
Stay, please stay on earth with us.
All of us are willing to be your loyal subjects,
We'll worship you throughout the seasons,
More devoutly than worshiping our ancestors.

YI (*Turns to* CHANG E.) Look how lovely these common people are. They adore me.

PEOPLE O mighty god Yi! Our sons and grandsons will be your servants and slaves,
And our descendants will be loyal to your descendants for generations to come.

CHANG E Don't forget we still have to go back to Heaven!

Yi	Of course, I'm the guard of the Heavenly God, how could I not go back? I'm going to report to him how good his people on earth are.
People	O lord, please do not forsake your people. Let's all kneel and beg him in earnest! Great Yi, Holy Yi, The kindest and the most benevolent. Please, you must help us to the very end. There are ten burning suns in the sky, The rice sprouts have all dried up and died. There's nothing to eat or drink, How can we go on living?

[Yi *looks up at the sky. The hot suns are burning, the dragon chariot is roaring by and the sky is clear with no trace of cloud.*

Yi	Hello, you Sons of Heaven, have you finished? Listen, you get off the dragon chariot now! You hear me? This is Yi the Archer speaking!

[*The* Ten Suns *stick out their heads and take a peep at earth below.*

Ten Suns	Who's yelling and shrieking on earth? Someone who calls himself Yi the Archer. He says he's a god from Heaven. The guy who guards the Gate of Heaven. Ha ha ha! Ha ha ha!
Yi	I'm warning you one more time, stop fooling around! These are the red bow and white arrows given to me by the Heavenly God himself. Don't tell me you don't recognize them.
Ten Suns	We're sick and tired of that toy. It's for the birds. The guy's funny. It's like using a chicken feather as a warrant.

	It's so much fun riding on the dragon chariot. Come, you wanna whoop it up too? Ask the guy to drive the chariot! That's no fun. Tell him to pull the dragon's ass instead. Who's stronger? He or the dragon? What a bummer! Don't waste time talking to him. Away—
YI	I'm giving you one last warning! The Heavenly God has given me a mandate to kill anyone who resists! (*Puts an arrow in place and bends his bow.*)
CHANG E	Yi, you must be out of your mind. They're all Sons of Heaven. You mustn't touch them—
YI	(*Pushes CHANG E away.*) I don't care who they are! I've got orders from the Heavenly God to quell the unrest. Now get off the dragon chariot, all of you, and go back to Sunrise Valley in Sweet Pool!
	[*PEOPLE move away from YI and back off.*
TEN SUNS	Drive on! Away! Away! Away! Eat the dragon's fart!
	[*The dragon chariot roars amid rolling clouds and blinding smoke.*
YI	Here comes an arrow!
	[*A black-feathered coat drifts down. PEOPLE scream in horror and scatter in all directions.*
CHANG E	My goodness! What a heinous crime!
	[*The SUNS turn the chariot around and drive it toward YI.*
THE SUNS	Hit him! Crush him dead! Hit him! Crush him dead! Crush him dead! Crush him dead!
	[*YI shoots another arrow. One more feather coat drifts down.*

CHANG E	(*Holding* YI.) Stop this madness! I beg you—
THE SUNS	Crush him to pieces! Crush him to pieces! Crush him to pieces! Crush him to pieces! Crush! Crush! Crush!—Crush him into powder!
YI	(*Pushes* CHANG E *away.*) One more arrow for the road!
	[*Another feather coat falls.*
CHANG E	Stop shooting! They're all Sons of Heaven!
THE SUNS	Crush—him—dead—!
YI	Take that!
	[*One more feather coat falls.*
CHANG E	(*Wailing.*) The Heavenly God will never forgive us. You've ruined me and you've ruined yourself …
THE SUNS	Give us back our brothers! Give us back our brothers! Give us back our brothers! Catch that murderer! Catch him, quick!
	[YI *laughs loudly. He turns and shoots another arrow. One more feather coat falls.*
CHANG E	(*To* PEOPLE.) He's gone totally mad. Stop him! Only you can stop him. He did all this to save you. None of you have said a word, why?
THE SUNS	Murderer! Murderer! Abominable murderer! We mustn't let him get away! Don't let him get away!
	[YI *spreads his legs and shoots another arrow. One more feather coat falls.* YI *laughs heartily.*
CHANG E	(*To* PEOPLE.) You pushed him to do all this, but now you're backing off. Cowards, all cowards, I curse you! Despicable pigs! (*Kneels down.*) Heavenly God, please forgive him.… What a catastrophe …

Yi	(*He pursues the suns as if he were mad. Shoots another arrow.*) Another feather.
	[*Another Sun drops dead.*
Three Suns	Mother, oh mother, please come quick! Come and save your children! This guy has gone mad, and he's gonna kill us all. (*They scurry in all directions.*)
Yi	There's no place to hide, you punks! Another feather! (*Shoots another arrow.*)
	[*A Sun drops dead.*
Two Suns	Please—don't—kill—us—
Yi	Take another feather. (*Shoots another arrow.*)
	[*Another Sun drops dead. The only remaining Sun takes off his feather coat and transforms himself into a Sun.*
Sun	In the name of the Heavenly God, please, please stop and spare me! Let me return to Sunrise Valley, okay?
Yi	(*Disengages the arrow from the bow.*) All right, I'll spare you so that you can report to the Heavenly God. Tell him that I've killed nine of your brothers, and that I'll return to the Celestial Court and be at his service again once I've restored peace on earth.
	[*Exit Sun dejected. People gradually form a circle around Yi.*
Yi	People, you saw what happened with your own eyes. All of you can be my witnesses. It was the gang of Sons of Heaven who disrupted the peace on earth. I relayed to them the Heavenly God's order, once, twice, three times. Of course they could quite easily ignore me, but I cannot allow anyone, not even the Sons of Heaven, to desecrate the sacred weapon bestowed on me by Heaven. That was why the feathers fell from

	the sky. The scorching heat has subsided and the rain is falling. From now on, all of you can live normal lives. And Yi has not been remiss in carrying out his duties.
PEOPLE	We all saw what happened. We'll bear witness to what happened. What you did was good for us. Now we can all go on living. You're a good god from Heaven. You're our savior! We'll be forever grateful, for thousands of generations to come! We'll burn incense every day and kneel to pay homage. The smoke will drift up to the Celestial Court, The Heavenly God will know and understand: It's you who got rid of those menaces for the people.
YI	(*To* CHANG E.) Get up, my dear. Let's go back to Heaven together and report to the Heavenly God. I'll take responsibility for everything I've done.

[*Exeunt* YI *and* CHANG E.

Enter SUN MOTHER *ceremoniously, followed by* ABLE EMPEROR.

SUN MOTHER	Give me back my sons! How can you be so heartless? For the power and glory of your rule, you're willing to kill your own sons! Why didn't you kill me as well? Tell that murderer Yi to come here. Tell him to shoot me dead with his arrow right in front of you! He might just as well. I'll die in front of you!
ABLE EMPEROR	Where's that criminal?
SUN MOTHER	Such a hypocrite! If you're tired of me, why didn't you say so earlier? Then I wouldn't have given birth to so many sons.... If you didn't like them, I could have taken them away, far away from here, but you didn't have to be so vicious....

ABLE EMPEROR	My dear wife, stop crying, will you? I must punish this murderer! (*Strikes his dragon-head scepter on the ground.*)
	[*Enter* TREE GOD GOU MANG, *one of the gods in Heaven. He has the face of a man and the body of a bird.*
TREE GOD	Gou Mang, the God of Tree and Life, at Your Majesty's service.
ABLE EMPEROR	Arrest that insolent villain and bring him back here to me!
TREE GOD	(*Looks round.*) Your Majesty, he's here already.
	[*Enter* YI *and* CHANG E. *They stand outside the Gate of Heaven.*
YI	(*Looks up toward the Celestial Court.*) Yi wishes to report to His Majesty.
	[CHANG E *is on her knees, her head lowered.*
YI	(*Drops to his knees and presents the monsters' flesh with both hands.*) Carrying out the Heavenly God's orders, I slaughtered Chiseled Teeth in the wilds of Farmland Flower, killed Nine-Headed Monster on Rough Water, slayed the Big Wind Peacock at Green Hill Pool, butchered Ya Yu and hacked Long Snake to pieces at Cave Court Lake, and vanquished Big Pig in Mulberry Grove. The Ten Suns were scorching the earth. They were the perpetrators of disaster. I had no choice but to shoot down nine of them. The earth is now peaceful and the people do not have to live in fear anymore. Allow me to present you with the monsters' flesh for your culinary enjoyment.
ABLE EMPEROR	Do you realize you're guilty as well?
YI	Your Majesty may decide at his discretion whether I'm guilty or successful in discharging my duties.

ABLE EMPEROR	(*Muttering.*) The people on earth adore you and want you to be their king. Why have you come back?
YI	Yi is a god in Heaven under your command.
ABLE EMPEROR	(*Striking his scepter.*) You have no place in the Celestial Court!
CHANG E	Please, Heavenly God, please have mercy and pity this poor little woman. Forgive him this once, keep him by my side, even if he has to sweep and clean the Celestial Court. Just give him a chance to redeem himself.
SUN MOTHER	I, Sun Mother, can't forgive him! I'm the first wife of the Heavenly God, mother of the Sons of Heaven, and I'll never forgive this brutal and bloodthirsty murderer!
ABLE EMPEROR	Enough, enough. Please cry no more.
	[*Exeunt the* ABLE EMPEROR *and* SUN MOTHER, *who is helped along by the* ABLE EMPEROR. TREE GOD *closes the Gate of Heaven and exit.*
YI	Well, the Gate of Heaven has been closed.
	[YI *gets up, turns and looks around, not knowing what to do.* CHANG E *weeps, her hands covering her face.*
	Enter STORYTELLER. *He has removed his face mask, which he now holds in his hand.*
CHANG E	Yi, what are your plans now? Don't be so down on yourself. Since the Heavenly God doesn't want you to serve him, why don't you go down and be a king on earth?
	[YI *embraces* CHANG E. *Exeunt both.*
	Curtain.

Act II

[*Enter* STORYTELLER *beating a big bamboo cylinder.*]

STORYTELLER Ladies and gentlemen, we're finished with the East side, so let's go and take a look at the South.

Flame Emperor, God of Agriculture, rules South Heaven; he doesn't like listening to birdsong. Calm and relaxed, he is aged and bent. He has only a young daughter, who stays by his side all day long.

Unexpectedly, there appears on the scene the restless and presumptuous Chi You, and the world becomes embroiled in turmoil once more. (*Exit.*)

[*Enter* FLAME EMPEROR, *God of Agriculture, wobbling. He has the face of an ox and the body of a human. His face is scarlet.* DOLLY, *his daughter, is helping him along.*]

DOLLY Father, ten women shamans have come up to Heaven from earth. They all seek an audience with you.

FLAME EMPEROR (*Sits down.*) Let them in.

[*Enter* TEN WOMEN SHAMANS *carrying exotic flowers and fruit.*]

TEN WOMEN SHAMANS Your Majesty, we're the Ten Women Shamans of Soul Mountain. Our names are Shaman Xian, Shaman Ji, Shaman Fen, Shaman Peng, Shaman Gu, Shaman

	Zhen, Shaman Li, Shaman Di, Shaman Xie and Shaman Luo. We've collected a hundred medicinal plants for your approval.
FLAME EMPEROR	Tell me, what kinds of wonderful things have you collected?
SHAMAN XIAN	Your Majesty, there's a mountain called Small Blossom in the West. I don't know whether you've heard of it. On the mountain, one can find a plant called a Bi Li.
FLAME EMPEROR	What? Bi Li? What a strange name.
SHAMAN XIAN	That's correct, Your Majesty. This plant grows either on tree trunks or inside the cracks of the rocks. It can be eaten to cure heart pain.
DOLLY	My father doesn't suffer from this ailment, do you, father?
FLAME EMPEROR	Of course not. I may be old, but I don't have such illnesses.
SHAMAN JI	In the West there's another mountain called Tally Ape, on which grows a tree known as Striped Tree. Its fruit is like dates and it can cure deafness.
DOLLY	My father's not deaf!
SHAMAN JI	Your Highness, this mountain also has a plant which looks like a mallow. It has scarlet flowers and the fruit is like a baby's tongue. After eating it, people won't suffer from delusions.
DOLLY	I'd like to be deluded, if only once. To see what it's like.
SHAMAN FEN	Your Highness, you're so sweet. Let me tell you what I've found. In the West, on Mount Yu Ci, I saw a bird which has a body like that of an owl, but it has a human face and only one leg. It's called a Tuo Fei. As soon as

	summer arrives, it hides itself and sleeps for a long time. Not until winter will it surface and be seen again. If a person eats this bird, he'll be rid of his fear of thunder.
DOLLY	(*Smiles.*) You can ask my father. Am I afraid of thunder?
FLAME EMPEROR	She plays hide-and-seek with Thunder God.
SHAMAN PENG	That goes without saying. What a joke it would be if the daughter of the Heavenly Emperor were afraid of thunder! Your Majesty, I actually went to Heavenly Emperor Mountain, which was of course named after Your Majesty. There was this bird flying toward me. It looked a lot like a quail, with black markings and a scarlet ruff. It's called a Li. Eating it will cure old people of piles.
FLAME EMPEROR	Perfect. It so happens that I'm suffering from this ailment. Leave the bird for me. All right, what else?
SHAMAN GU	In the northwest there's also a mountain called the Incomplete Mountain. River water bubbles up from underneath it continuously. At the summit there's a wonderful fruit tree. Its leaves are like those of date trees but the fruit is as big as a peach. When someone eats it, he forgets all about tiredness.
FLAME EMPEROR	That's a great tonic. Save it for me.
SHAMAN ZHEN	Your Highness, in the West there's also Pinecone Mountain. There's a bird there called a Wagtail. It looks like a mountain fowl, with a black body and red feet. The meat is good for your skin and prevents wrinkles.
DOLLY	I don't even have a trace of a wrinkle.
FLAME EMPEROR	You might as well keep that for yourself. Anything else?
SHAMAN LI	Your Majesty, further to the West is Mount Brave Boot,

	where the lacquer trees are plentiful. The foot of the mountain is strewn with gold and jade, and on the mountain the birds and animals are white all over. The Meandering River starts from there and flows north to Hill Ram Marsh. They say that the water provides nutrition for a strange fish called a Ran Yi. The fish has a snake's head and six feet, and its eyes are as big as a horse's ears. After eating it, people won't have any more nightmares. Will it be of any use to Your Highness?
DOLLY	I just want to know … if there are any plants that'll make me more attractive?
SHAMAN DI	Of course there are. There are all kinds of wonderful things on earth. What you want is something called Jade Grass! It's found on Sister-in-law Mountain. The leaves are folded and the flowers are yellow. Its fruit is like dodder seeds. After eating the fruit, a woman will become irresistibly attractive. Whoever sees her will be captivated by her charms.
DOLLY	That's it. I only want this Jade Grass. I don't want anything else.
FLAME EMPEROR	Not even your father?
DOLLY	Father, I didn't mean that!
FLAME EMPEROR	I know, I know. Your father knows everything. All right, let's talk about something else. You shamans are all very knowledgeable. So tell us some strange happenings overseas. I don't want my daughter to get bored.
SHAMAN XIE	Your Majesty, there's a country called Protruding Chest Country. Has Your Highness ever heard about it? The people in this country all have chicken's chests. When they walk, their arms are tucked in at the back

Act II ■ 39

	like birds' wings. The birds in this place have one wing, one eye and one foot. They can't move an inch. So the male and female have to pair up to fly. That's why they're called Side-by-Side Birds.
DOLLY	This place sounds no fun at all.
SHAMAN LUO	Your Highness, in the East there's a country called Reversed Tongue Country. The people's tongues are rolled up backward and they talk likewise. For example, when they greet each other, they don't say "How are you?" but "You are how?" instead. You might think that they're actually cursing people. You have to reverse their words in order to understand them.
DOLLY	Father, that country sounds quite fun.
SHAMAN XIAN	Your Highness, let me tell you about another country in the East. There everybody dresses neatly and properly and carries a beautiful sword at the waist. They also have two tigers, as docile as the cats in your house, who follow them around, one on the left and one on the right. People there never get into quarrels or fights. That's why the country is called Gentlemen Country. Oh yes, and the place is strewn with beautiful blooming flowers.
SHAMAN JI	Your Highness, in the East Sea area there's also a mountain called Bath Valley Mountain. Big People Country is to be found on this mountain, which is located in the middle of the sea. People there all enjoy talking and they're humorous speakers. They often host gatherings in a mirage on the surface of the sea. Unfortunately, you can only watch from a distance, you can't go near them.
DOLLY	Father, I want to go and play by the East Sea.

FLAME EMPEROR	(*Waving his hand.*) That's all for today. We'll call you if we need you.
TEN SHAMANS	Thank you for your hospitality, Your Majesty. (*Exeunt.*)
FLAME EMPEROR	My dear daughter, our Celestial Court is not that small and there are many gods here. Can't you find one who's to your liking?
DOLLY	Oh, those! They're so rude and so low. They all look like blockheads. To them winning is everything; all they do is brag in front of you to get rewards.
FLAME EMPEROR	There must be some who look like Prince Charming on earth, don't you think?
DOLLY	Those small-minded, calculating bootlickers? They're a total waste of time.
FLAME EMPEROR	Heaven may be big, but all the gods are under my jurisdiction. They all listen to my commands. Where else can you go to find someone you like?
DOLLY	That's why I have to go to the East Sea to look for someone who's not beholden to you, who is independent, strong-willed, handsome, unpretentious and loving. I don't care if he's a god or a man. I could live and die for him. That's what they call love. You don't understand, do you?
FLAME EMPEROR	Your father's getting old.
DOLLY	But father, your heart is not old at all.
FLAME EMPEROR	It's all because of sadness. When someone suffers from sadness, his heart gets old as a result.
DOLLY	I don't understand why I'm always so sad either. Father, am I going to get old soon?
FLAME EMPEROR	You've already set your mind on going to the East Sea, so go. You can relax by the seaside and perhaps you'll

	even find the man of your dreams. If that happens, you won't be sad any more. But bring him back to see me as soon as you can. Don't forget your old man.
DOLLY	Don't say things like that, father.
FLAME EMPEROR	Go! Go now.
	[*Exit* DOLLY.
FLAME EMPEROR	(*Stands up and looks around.*) Take a look at my old friend in the East. His nine sons died one after the other. He must be overwhelmed with sadness. He's probably weaker than I and walks with difficulty … spending all his time listening to the birds singing in the bamboo grove. (*Shakes his head.*) But then there's peace in the East. (*Turns to look.*) The Kun Lun Mountains in the West are so murky and indistinct. I can't see them clearly. It must be these eyes of mine. They're old and they're failing me. (*Claps his hands.*)
	[*Enter* CHI YOU. *He has the face of a human, the body of an animal and the hoofs of an ox. His head is of copper and his eyes are fiery.*
CHI YOU	What is Your Majesty's wish?
FLAME EMPEROR	The Kun Lun Mountains are always covered in clouds and mist. Chi You, take a good look and see what my old neighbor Queen Mother of the West is doing.
CHI YOU	Is Your Majesty talking about the crouching tigress inside the rocky cave on Jasper Lake, the one living on Jade Mountain?
FLAME EMPEROR	She must be very old, so old that her teeth have all fallen out.
CHI YOU	Look. Three red-headed, three-footed crows have flown there from Three Dangers Mountain.

FLAME EMPEROR	Those are the Three Blue Birds. They look for all kinds of food and bring them to Queen Mother of the West. You mean she's still as insatiable as ever? In the good old days if she wished to take a bite out of some man, she would actually swallow him, bones and all.
CHI YOU	Looks like she's eating a peach.
FLAME EMPEROR	It must be one of those long-life peaches. They make people immortal. She eats everything, the fresher the merrier. But this old tigress can only eat peaches now—her teeth have probably all fallen out. Let her eat all the peaches she wants.
CHI YOU	Your Majesty, look. A huge palace has suddenly appeared east of the Kun Lun Mountains. The fences surrounding it are all made of jade. There are nine wells and nine big doors on each side, guarded by none other than the tiger-headed, human-faced Bright Beasts.
FLAME EMPEROR	Make sure you're not seeing things.
CHI YOU	Your Majesty, with due respect, my eyes are made of gold and fire, and they can penetrate the darkest clouds and see through the densest fog. I can clearly see the towering Kun Lun Mountains covered with Rice Trees, which are sixty feet tall and five arm spans round. To the west of the Bright Beasts there are Phoenixes and Wonder Birds with serpents on their heads and at their feet. With due respect, Your Majesty, there couldn't be any mistake. To the north of the Bright Beasts, there's the divine Scarlet Bird. It's as red as flaming fire, and it's responsible for guarding the Grow-Back Meat, which regenerates itself after being eaten, and the Treasure Tree with its vast store of pearls and precious jade. So regal and majestic!
FLAME EMPEROR	Look further!

CHI YOU	East of the Bright Beasts, six shamans are holding Ya Yu's corpse and forcing a no-death drug into his mouth to revive him!
FLAME EMPEROR	Ya Yu was killed by the Heavenly God Twin Load and his minister Peril, wasn't that right?
CHI YOU	Your Majesty, take a look. Twin Load and Peril have bound together and hung upside down from a tree! The tree is to the northwest of the Bright Beasts—
FLAME EMPEROR	This is really bizarre! That was nothing but a personal squabble between the gods—who'd have wasted his time taking on the role of adjudicator?
CHI YOU	Who else but the Yellow Emperor of the North? The Able Emperor of the East spends all his time listening to the birds sing, the Queen Mother of the West only cares about eating peaches, and your mind is set on enjoying your sunset years. You might as well let Yellow Emperor gang up with the gods and take over your kingdom. Just wait and see, Your Majesty!
FLAME EMPEROR	Are you sure that the Kun Lun Mountains have become Yellow Emperor's capital on earth?
CHI YOU	His son Yu Hao is already the god of the East Sea, and the North Sea is now governed by his grandson, Yu Jing. Are you going to just sit here and let him gobble up all the land on earth? You're a heavenly emperor and you have your dignity and pride. How are you going to face your people and your kingdom?
FLAME EMPEROR	I'm getting on in years. I don't want to wage any war.
CHI YOU	Your Majesty, where's your honor? Are you willing to serve under Yellow Emperor and obey his orders just like that?
FLAME EMPEROR	This is no small matter. I'll have to consider it carefully.

CHI YOU	Your Majesty, in Chi You's family are seventy-two brothers, all of them as strong as oxen, what are you afraid of? Besides, you have Big Talk in the North, Gong Gong in the South, and don't forget Headless the Reckless. Which god in Heaven would dare to disobey your orders?
FLAME EMPEROR	I just want to live in peace with everybody, and the Celestial Court to be a restful place for all.
CHI YOU	Then rest all you want. I'm not going to sit here and do nothing, waiting for him to hang me upside down from a tree and chop my head off! (*Exit CHI YOU in anger.*)
FLAME EMPEROR	He's gone, the impetuous fool. (*Sound of an ox horn.*) No more peace on earth! (*Claps his hands. Stops. Then claps his hands once more.*) Nobody pays any attention to me any more. Everybody has run away, leaving this lonely old man behind. Not even my little girl is here with me. What am I saying? She's gone to the East Sea! Maybe I've lost it. Come! Find my daughter and bring her back to me! (*Exit.*)
	[*Enter STORYTELLER, beating a copper gong.*
STORYTELLER	The gods in Heaven are hustling, Busy making preparations for war. Yi has been banished from Heaven, Wandering around to kill time. Chang E had a quarrel with her husband, The two are sleeping in separate beds. Down and out, Yi meets the River Lord's wife On the shore of the Luo River. A disheartened hero meets By chance an abandoned wife. Needless to say, An amorous encounter is about to take place.

[*Enter Yi and Fu Fei separately.*]

Yi (*Comes to a halt.*) What an exquisite beauty!

Storyteller (*Moving in between Yi and Fu Fei.*) What charming and lingering eyes! And yet so full of sorrow. Whoever sees her, his heart will surely start pounding. Even the gods in Heaven are no exception. (*Exit.*)

Yi Hey, beautiful. How come you look so sad and worried? Why are you roaming by the river all alone? I hope you're not thinking of doing yourself in!

Fu Fei Stranger, hold your tongue. Just go away! I'm telling you this for your own good. Don't bring trouble upon yourself.

Yi (*Laughs.*) Trouble? How does it taste? Is it as sweet as honey?

Fu Fei Stop your teasing or you may find it's too late for repentance.

Yi Repentance? How does that taste? Is it sweet or sour?

Fu Fei Stop flirting, and don't make goo-goo eyes at me. You're good-looking and very talented. Don't get yourself killed over a woman.

Yi Your tearful eyes, you're saying that they're as sharp and dangerous as a sword?

Fu Fei I can hear his footsteps already. Go quick. Go! He'll kill you!

Yi Who are you talking about? Your husband or your lover?

Fu Fei I'm only one among his countless number of women. He has a new one every day.

Yi Let me guess, he's a brutal robber who kills people without blinking an eye. Or is he an imperious

	overlord, a tyrant who indulges in unbridled debauchery?
Fu Fei	He's even worse than robbers and overlords. Please, I beg you, please go and hide.
Yi	Why don't you run away?
Fu Fei	Of course I want to! But I can't escape from his iron grip …
Yi	Beautiful lady, you just have to give me the nod and I'll take you away this very moment!
Fu Fei	You're very kind. But you don't understand. I really can't—
Yi	Woman, thy name is enigma. Even the gods can't figure you out.
Fu Fei	Please don't toy with me. I'm in no mood for fun and games.…
Yi	Which makes you even more charming and delicate.… Let me tell you, I'm not a crook or a criminal. Why do you refuse my helping hand?
Fu Fei	Run, quick … oh no, it's too late!
	[*Enter* River Lord. *He has a white dragon's head, a human body and sharp claws.*]
River Lord	Shameless rascal! How dare you flirt with my wife in broad daylight! (*Jumps on* Yi.)
Fu Fei	Don't kill him! Don't kill him!
Yi	(*Gets his bow and arrow ready to shoot.*) I'm Yi the Archer, the God of Power. Who do you think you are?
	[*The* River Lord *gives a strange cry, covers his left eye, stumbles and falls to the ground, then gets up and flees. Exit running.* Yi *laughs loudly, his face toward the sky.*

Fu Fei	I know you. Aren't you the hero who slaughtered Chiseled Teeth, killed Nine-Headed Monster, brought down Big Wind Peacock, killed Big Pig, shot Ya Yu and cut up Long Snake?
Yi	You're looking at him.
Fu Fei	You're Yi the Archer, the God of Power who shot down the nine suns? The one who was then banished from the Celestial Court?
Yi	The very same. Forget about the one-eyed demon and follow me. Let's take a trip together, let's go to the edge of the sky and the end of the world! We'll have so much fun!
Fu Fei	But I ... I can't, I really can't....
Yi	You can't go or you can't not go.... Make up your mind. Ah, women!
Fu Fei	I'm a water goddess. I can't leave the banks of the Luo River.
Yi	You're a water goddess, not a water plant. Why must you stick with the river all the time? Why can't you go away with me?
Fu Fei	You just don't understand, do you? Once I leave the Luo River, I'll instantly become pale and haggard. My beauty and youth will fade like fleeting clouds and smoke.
Yi	So you're asking me to rub shoulders with fish and prawns in the water? People will laugh their heads off.
Fu Fei	Don't say that, my good Yi. Once you take leave of the hustle and bustle of the human world, you'll enjoy yourself in the good company of Fu Fei in the Crystal Palace in the water. It may not be as magnificent as

the Celestial Court, but it's exquisite and translucent, and the scenery is quite extraordinary. I'll ask Hill Fish and Mottled Fish to dance for you. And of course there is me, Fu Fei, who will make love to you all day and all night. I promise that you'll be able to put all your pains and troubles behind you.

YI I was born a god in Heaven. How could I confine myself in this tiny water country?

FU FEI Don't be silly. My good Yi, you've killed so many Sons of Heaven, how will the Heavenly God be able to forgive you? Take my advice, stop roaming the world and enjoy yourself in the realm of love and tenderness. Are you afraid that you won't be able to forget Chang E? Come on. That goddess was banished from Heaven all on your account. You can't really blame her for the animosity she has shown toward you. Where else will you be able to find the affection I have for you? Besides, the wife may be beautiful, but she can't compete with the seductive and tempting mistress.

[YI *stares intently at* FU FEI *and picks her up in his arms. Exeunt.*]

Enter STORYTELLER *with a leather drum tied to his waist and a brass gong in his hand. He is beating the drum and the gong as he goes.*

STORYTELLER (*Sings.*)
The war between the Flame Emperor and the Yellow
    Emperor is fierce,
In haste, the Yellow Emperor takes on Chi You and
    they fight at the Wilderness of Deer Chasing.
Black Bear, Brown Bear, Tiger and Leopard are in the
    vanguard;
Blue Pheasant, Kite Bird and all kinds of eagles are his
    cover in the sky.

But Chi You has a brass head and a pair of flaming eyes,
He munches stones and sprays blinding sand from his mouth.
The Wind Master and Rain Chief are his aides;
They conjure up a thick fog to enshroud the entire sky.
And the gang of ghouls and goblins go on the rampage.
It is a bloodbath,
The gods and the ghosts screech and squeal,
And Heaven and earth turn dark and dim!

[*Enter* YELLOW EMPEROR, *leading* BLACK BEAR, BROWN BEAR, TIGER, LEOPARD, BLUE PHEASANT, KITE BIRD *and all kinds of eagles. The* YELLOW EMPEROR *is golden on all sides, front and back, left and right. In his hand is a precious sword.*

Enter CHI YOU, *leading* WIND MASTER *and* RAIN CHIEF *who are spraying mist from their mouths. On* CHI YOU's *order, a gang of spirits and demons enter and surround the* YELLOW EMPEROR *and his group. The two sides engage in a fierce battle.*

STORYTELLER (*Sings.*)
Ah, the Yellow Emperor,
A valiant fighter is he.
He battles on four sides,
All at the same time.
But with Chi You's onslaught,
He is not the one to match.
He has to run,
And run away quick.
In utter embarrassment,
He manages to escape.

[*Exit* YELLOW EMPEROR *scurrying away.*

STORYTELLER (*Stops beating his drum and gong and recites.*)

Myths can only be told as stories of the gods,
If you told them as human tales,
They'd just be jokes badly told.
Let the moralists find their morals,
And the philosophers their metaphysics.
Ladies and gentlemen of the audience,
You've come to the theater to watch a play,
You see people die, and you see people get hurt,
But it's all just make-believe. (*Exit.*)

[*Smoke dissipates. The* QUEEN MOTHER OF THE WEST *appears. She has the body of a human, the teeth of a tiger and the tail of a leopard. Her hair is disheveled and her face is grimy. She is also wearing jade headgear.*

Three three-footed BLUE BIRDS *fly down from the Everlasting Tree. The birds are like* GOLDEN CROWS. *They flap their wings to wake up the* QUEEN MOTHER.

She walks out of the cave in tiger steps, lifts her head toward the sky and lets out a lengthy howl.

QUEEN MOTHER   Who dares to disturb my sweet dreams?

[*The three* BLUE BIRDS *lift their wings one after another.*

QUEEN MOTHER   Bring me the culprit!

[*The three* BLUE BIRDS *hesitate and pull in their wings.*

QUEEN MOTHER   Who is it that has scared my Blue Birds so?

[*Enter* YI, *his hands empty.*

QUEEN MOTHER   Do you know what place this is?

YI   I think this must be the Jade Mountain in the Kun Lun range, in which is located the abode of the honorable Queen Mother of the West.

QUEEN MOTHER   How dare you barge in here uninvited and without my Blue Birds ushering you in?

Yi	I beg the Queen Mother's forgiveness. With all due respect, I have traversed the Flaming Mountain and crossed the Weak Water River in the abyss of Mount Surround to come here.
Queen Mother	Are you the same Power God Yi who guarded the Celestial Court? Come over here, let me take a look at you. Did you shoot down those birds from Heaven one after another?
Yi	I think I did.
Queen Mother	Don't you know that I have a no-death drug that can resurrect them from their death?
Yi	I know.
Queen Mother	Impetuous fool, what are you doing here? Don't you know that I can order people to live or die just like that? And that I not only possess the no-death drug but also control all kinds of plagues?
Yi	I know.
Queen Mother	And you're not afraid that I'll let out some disease that will knock you out right here on the spot?
Yi	Of course, I'm afraid. But I know that the Queen Mother's very kind and she wouldn't let me die.
Queen Mother	How'd you know that I'd be more kind-hearted than the Heavenly Emperor?
Yi	I only thought that you'd have mercy on me.
Queen Mother	Oh yes? Don't you know that I, Queen Mother of the West, have no mercy?
Yi	I know.
Queen Mother	But you still venture here, and you dare to take the tiger by the tail?

Yi	I have no intention of offending you. I've just come here to ask for your help.
Queen Mother	I know, I know. You want me to plead with the Heavenly Emperor to let you go back to the Celestial Court, right? You fully understand that you're dreaming, don't you?
Yi	I know you're not in the habit of pleading for anybody, and you don't ask favors of anybody. I just wanted to ask you …
Queen Mother	Ask me what?
Yi	I don't want my life to end just like that.
Queen Mother	Good grief! You've had enough of your fun and games, and now you want me to give you the no-death drug?
Yi	Yes, Queen Mother. I don't want to die like a mortal.
Queen Mother	I thought you were fearless even to the point of being impudent. But you're actually afraid of dying?
Yi	Before, I had nothing to fear because I was one of the gods in Heaven. Now I've been demoted to live in the human world, and death is getting closer and closer every day. But I haven't lived long enough.
Queen Mother	This is true. But don't you know that honesty can kill as well?
Yi	I was a god, and gods don't lie. I still haven't learned to lie like human beings.
Queen Mother	Even if I give you the no-death drug, it still won't save your life because you don't know how to lie.
Yi	But if I lied to you, d'you think you'd give me the no-death drug?
Queen Mother	You've got a point there. Fine, this no-death tree of

	mine blooms once every three thousand years and bears fruit once every six thousand years. I can only give you one piece. Don't let anybody know before you eat it. Particularly, you have to be aware of women, whether it's your mistress, that foxy water spirit, or your wife, the demoted goddess from Heaven. If a woman steals my fruit and eats it, she'll be transformed into a toad for sure! D'you hear me?
YI	Yes, ma'am.
QUEEN MOTHER	(*To BLUE BIRDS.*) Pick a no-death fruit for him. You've got to remember this: human beings are untrustworthy. That's why I've sent down a plague on them to punish them.
YI	And if I'm dishonest, you can also punish me in the same way.
QUEEN MOTHER	Fine. You can go now.
YI	(*Takes the no-death fruit.*) Thank you, Queen Mother.
	[*The QUEEN MOTHER lets out a lengthy howl, turns and disappears. Exit YI.*
	Enter YELLOW EMPEROR, his son the God of the East Sea YU HAO and his grandson the God of the North Sea YU JING, in a hurry. YU HAO has a human face and a bird's body, and two yellow NINE-HEADED MONSTERS curled around his ears and feet. YU JING also has a human face and a bird's body; two green NINE-HEADED MONSTERS are curled around his ears and two red NINE-HEADED MONSTERS are at his feet.
	Faint battle cries are heard.
YU HAO	Big Talk in the north and the Miao tribe in the south have been incited by Chi You to stir up trouble. One after another they've ganged up with the rebels. Even

	that ruthless son of a bitch Headless the Reckless has joined them. Father, it looks like the East Sea is going to be peaceful for the time being. Why don't you go and stay there for a while?
YELLOW EMPEROR	You're saying that I should relinquish control over the central plains? Then how am I going to get to my Celestial Court?
YU JING	Grandpa, Chi You and his gang can't swim. Let me lure them to the shore of the North Sea, and then I'll conjure up a gargantuan sky-high tidal wave and drown them, swallowing them up like dog meat.
YELLOW EMPEROR	Don't interrupt me. (*Hesitating for a moment.*) All the gods are sitting on the fence, waiting to see which side will emerge victorious. It looks like we'll have to mobilize the demons and spirits. I've heard that seven thousand miles from where your East Sea joins the ocean is Flowing Waves Mountain, home of the Giant Ox, and there's also Thunder Marsh, the place of Thunder Beast. They say that both of them know how to overcome Chi You. Could we ask them to come and help with the war?
YU HAO	They're very unruly, both of them, and they spend their time roaming between Heaven and earth. They've never supported or helped anyone in any war. Even if I went and invited them, I'm afraid they might not want to come.
YELLOW EMPEROR	Just tell them that I, the Heavenly Emperor, am holding a big feast and that they've been invited. Don't say a word about the war.
YU HAO	But this war has shaken Heaven and earth, who wouldn't know about it?
YELLOW EMPEROR	I'm known for my hospitality and I like to entertain.

	They should know that too. (*Waves his hand.*) Go now and come back quickly. Don't fail me!
	[*Exit* YU HAO *hurriedly.* YELLOW EMPEROR *paces around.*]
YELLOW EMPEROR	Yu Jing, you said you'd invited Winged Dragon. How come he's still not here yet?
YU JING	I've already asked him three or more times. Each time he said that he would come soon.
YELLOW EMPEROR	Kids are kids. You can never trust them. Did you or didn't you tell him clearly that it was I who'd invited him?
YU JING	The first time he said he'd come as soon as he'd finished brushing his teeth. The second time, he said he had to take a bath. And the third time, he was in the toilet, saying that since it was the Yellow Emperor who'd invited him he had to be clean inside and out.
YELLOW EMPEROR	That little fellow never fails to mess things up! (*Pacing to and fro.*) Go and see what your Auntie Aridity's doing. Tell her to come and see me at once.
YU JING	Yes, Grandpa. D'you think Winged Dragon will come? (*Exit.*)
	[*Enter* WINGED DRAGON. *He has a dragon's head and body, with a pair of wings.*]
WINGED DRAGON	Your Majesty, talk of Winged Dragon and Winged Dragon is here.
YELLOW EMPEROR	Please be seated.
WINGED DRAGON	I wouldn't dare sit on the throne of the Yellow Emperor.
YELLOW EMPEROR	Just sit down. Sit.
	[WINGED DRAGON *sits down.* YELLOW EMPEROR *continues to pace around.*]

YELLOW EMPEROR	You can see that Chi You's making a lot of trouble. But you still refuse to lend me a hand. Why?
WINGED DRAGON	Your Majesty, you know as well as I do, I have no quarrel with Chi You.
YELLOW EMPEROR	You're scared to death of his brass head and flaming eyes, aren't you?
WINGED DRAGON	Not at all! Your Majesty, you're surrounded by so many capable heavenly gods and generals, why would you need me to fight your war?
YELLOW EMPEROR	This is a good chance for you to show off your talents. Right now, who in the universe hasn't heard of Chi You? Even his helpers, the Wind Master and the Rain Chief, who have been conjuring up wind and rain to help him, have become well-known celebrities. Tell me, who knows whether Winged Dragon is a snake or a dragon god? And who knows that you, too, can turn on your magical powers and conjure up wind and rain?
WINGED DRAGON	No doubt, these two tricks are worth seeing. I can also turn a river or an ocean upside down, and suck up all the water in the East Sea and then spit it out again! Wind Master and Rain Chief, who do they think they are? They're not in my league.
YELLOW EMPEROR	Talent unused is talent wasted. You can boast all you want about your magical powers, but if you don't use them, it's the same as not having them.
WINGED DRAGON	If I used all my magical powers, Your Majesty's Heaven would be engulfed in pitch darkness.
YELLOW EMPEROR	Are you sure you possess that kind of talent?
WINGED DRAGON	Your Majesty underestimates me.
YELLOW EMPEROR	If you're really that talented, why don't you join my

	retinue and be my bodyguard from now on? What do you say?
WINGED DRAGON	Your Majesty, you just watch how I, Winged Dragon, take care of this stupid son of a bitch Chi You! (*Jumps down from the throne.*)
YELLOW EMPEROR	(*Throws down his sword.*) Yu Jing, escort Winged Dragon into battle!

[*Yu Jing picks up the sword. Exit with* WINGED DRAGON.

Enter YELLOW EMPEROR's *daughter* ARIDITY. *She is dressed in green and has her hair in a bun.*

ARIDITY	Father, from the moment I was born, I've hardly ever seen you, let alone received any gift from you. I'm ugly, I know, but ugly or not, I'm still your daughter, your own flesh and blood.
YELLOW EMPEROR	Don't be impudent! I'm not as muddled as that old fool Able Emperor. He did everything to spoil his children and in the end he only managed to kill them. You were born a Daughter of Heaven, but you still have to achieve something yourself. Otherwise, the gods will say that I'm unjust and unwise in meting out rewards and punishments, and that we're all lazy by nature. Imagine what the Celestial Court would be like then! Now every one of us is busy fighting Chi You and you can't just idle your time away and do nothing. I'm sending you to assist Winged Dragon to clear the fog conjured up by Wind Master and Rain Chief. As soon as you've proven yourself in battle, you'll have face and people will respect you for it.
ARIDITY	You used to hide me away. You didn't want me to see anybody. But now you're asking me to fight on the battlefield and show my face to the world. Aren't you afraid that you'll be embarrassed by your bald-

	headed daughter, and then the whole world will laugh at you, and you'll lose your dignity among the people?
YELLOW EMPEROR	Aridity, mark my words! A woman's beauty brings not happiness but disaster. Have you ever seen a beautiful woman who has a happy ending to her story?
ARIDITY	I'd rather endure the pains of being a woman than be disgusting and repulsive.
YELLOW EMPEROR	Don't talk to your father like that! You're the Daughter of Heaven and you don't need to use your feminine charm to make people like you. You only have to wield your power a little and the people will crawl at your feet! My good girl, hold your head up high. You can summon winds and you can cause a drought across the land for a thousand miles. Who in the whole wide world would dare laugh at you? Quite the opposite. They have to bow to you, they have to prostrate themselves in fear before you and burn incense to pay you homage. The people, I know them only too well.

[*Enter* YU HAO *running and panting.*

YU HAO	Father, Thunder Beast and Giant Ox are here.
YELLOW EMPEROR	(*To* ARIDITY.) Leave me. I'm busy working out a strategy for the war. See you on the battlefield.

[*Exit* ARIDITY. *Enter* THUNDER BEAST *and* GIANT OX. THUNDER BEAST *has a human head and a dragon's body. His belly is enormous.* GIANT OX *has a grayish body like a buffalo, but he is hornless and has only one foot.*

YELLOW EMPEROR	(*Moves up to welcome them.*) Welcome, welcome, honored guests. You have come a long way. Have you both come from the edge of Heaven?
THUNDER BEAST	We didn't think it would be proper to decline Your Majesty's hospitality.

GIANT OX	Your Majesty has a multitude of official duties to attend to. We're flattered to have been invited.
YELLOW EMPEROR	This is different. You've had to cross the sea on one foot. My apologies if I've inconvenienced you and made you come on a tiring journey. Please take the seat of honor.
GIANT OX	I'm used to being in the sea. I don't feel right when I'm out of the water. I think I'd better bend my leg and squat down on my heel.
YELLOW EMPEROR	Then may I ask Thunder Beast to take the seat of honor?
THUNDER BEAST	By no means. Your Majesty, please take the seat yourself. With a belly like mine, it's better to move around as much as possible.
YELLOW EMPEROR	Fine then. (*Takes the seat.*) Son, serve our guests some wine.
	[*Exit Yu Hao.*]
YELLOW EMPEROR	My unworthy son here is in charge of the East Sea. Fortunately you two have been kind enough to give him your strongest support. So today I've invited you here to express my gratitude.
THUNDER BEAST	Your Majesty flatters us. Actually the feeling is mutual. In this way, we can look after one another.
	[*Enter Yu Hao, carrying divine nectar, with which he fills Thunder Beast's and Giant Ox's cups.*]
GIANT OX	(*Smells the drink again and again.*) I've never tried anything like this.
YELLOW EMPEROR	The wonders of the sea of course are not worth mentioning to you two gentlemen, but this drink is something new. Just to show my appreciation.

YU HAO	This nectar was made from the fruits of pearl and jade grown on the Yu Qi trees on the top of the Kun Lun Mountains in the West. The water was the sweet spring water found at the foot of the Kun Lun Mountains.
THUNDER BEAST	(*Tasting.*) Only in Heaven!
GIANT OX	Wonderful bouquet.
YU HAO	This is made exclusively for father. Even the gods in Heaven rarely get the chance to taste it.
YELLOW EMPEROR	Please, gentlemen, make yourselves at home. (*Signals YU HAO to serve more drink.*) Your magical powers are known far and wide. I've heard about them countless times. Now that you're here, and we have this wonderful wine to add to the festivities, please tell me about them. I've heard that if you make your huge belly go up and down a bit, deafening thunderclaps are heard in the sky.
THUNDER BEAST	I wouldn't wish to be disrespectful.
YELLOW EMPEROR	We rarely get the chance to meet. Let's enjoy ourselves now that we're together.
THUNDER BEAST	Since Your Majesty insists, I'm happy to oblige. I respectfully beg your indulgence. (*He taps his stomach lightly with his finger. Immediately a thunderclap is heard.*)
	[*Everyone bursts out laughing.*
YELLOW EMPEROR	(*Half rising from his seat.*) Please, have some more.
	[THUNDER BEAST *and* GIANT OX *drink again.*
YELLOW EMPEROR	People say that you're like a god, Giant Ox. Whenever you go in or out of the water, there's great wind and rain, and flashing lightning and roaring thunder. Is that really true?
GIANT OX	I wouldn't want to be insolent with Your Majesty.

	It's not right to be contemptuous of the Celestial Court.
THUNDER BEAST	We both know our places. We've never been presumptuous or tried to be number one. Once in a while, we'd help to rein in those monsters which are disrespectful toward the gods of Heaven, or to manage the ordinary people. We haven't been involved in any fighting among the gods in Heaven. We just want to stay out of trouble.
GIANT OX	I couldn't agree more. We live at the edge of Heaven and beyond the sea, and we enjoy being free and easy.
YELLOW EMPEROR	I've always been like that too. I promote peace and harmony. If everyone in Heaven and on earth were like the two of you, we would have no need for war!
	[*Everybody bursts out laughing.*]
YELLOW EMPEROR	(*Facing YU HAO.*) My son has been put in charge of the East Sea. He could certainly use your support in the future.
	[YU HAO *moves forward and pours wine from the bottle for the guests.*]
GIANT OX	Thank you. Thank you very much.
THUNDER BEAST	Thank you. Let me serve myself.
GIANT OX	This nectar … it gets stronger the more you drink it.
THUNDER BEAST	You shouldn't drink too much, but then again, you can't help drinking it.
GIANT OX	It grows on you …
YELLOW EMPEROR	(*Sits up straight and becomes serious.*) Oh yes, I have something that I would like to discuss with you.
THUNDER BEAST	Your humble servant is all ears.

GIANT OX	My pleasure!
YELLOW EMPEROR	I want to make a big drum—
THUNDER BEAST	Excellent idea!
GIANT OX	How big?
YELLOW EMPEROR	For example.... Let me put it this way.... You, Giant Ox, if I used your skin to make the drumhead, and you, Thunder Beast, if I employed your thighbones as drumsticks, I would be able to create the most powerful music in the world when I beat the drum, wouldn't I?
THUNDER BEAST	(*Jumps up in shock.*) What did you say—(*His knees go weak, and he drops down and kneels on the ground.*)
GIANT OX	What ... what did he say?
YELLOW EMPEROR	It's my wish to borrow your skin and your bones.
GIANT OX	How ... how ... can you ...
THUNDER BEAST	Borrow?
YELLOW EMPEROR	The Yellow Emperor attempts what others deem impossible. Why should I try something that others can do? I'm the Heavenly Emperor, how can I just borrow axes and rice like ordinary folk? Now I have to defeat the rebellious Chi You, and since you two gentlemen are unwilling to cooperate, I'm afraid I'll have to put you to some inconvenience.
THUNDER BEAST	If this isn't murder ... then what is? (*He is unable to support himself and falls down.*)
YELLOW EMPEROR	(*Laughs loudly.*) Murder, really? I treated you like VIPs and we discussed the matter in an open and frank manner. I would rather call it a consultation.
GIANT OX	Has anyone ever seen this kind of ... consultation? (*He tries to get up but fails.*)

THUNDER BEAST	Conspiracy …
YELLOW EMPEROR	I, Yellow Emperor, have always been completely open and above board! I don't mind telling you now. When all this is over I'll make sure that your names are remembered and your meritorious deeds are known far and wide. Gentlemen, allow me to propose a toast to you as a gesture of my gratitude. You're deities, you should act like gods. Thunder Beast, set a good example! Son, fill their cups for them.

[THUNDER BEAST *and* GIANT OX *drink up in fear and then slump down abruptly. Exit* YELLOW EMPEROR.

Enter Yu JING *in a hurry. He and Yu* HAO *drag away the bodies of* THUNDER BEAST *and* GIANT OX *together.*

Enter CHANG E. *She looks around.*

STORYTELLER *follows her at a distance. In his left hand he is carrying an earthenware jar and in his right he is holding a chopstick. He beats the jar once.*

CHANG E	(*Seeing no one, she stops worrying.*) He must still be fasting. (*Ponders.*) Poor Chang E, you've been demoted to earth, and you have to stay in the house all day and bore yourself to death. That husband of yours, he goes out for ages, and when he comes home, he doesn't speak so much as a word. Then you have to wait on him while he takes a bath, and burn incense for him so that he can pray. If he had known that he should respect the Heavenly Emperor, he wouldn't have— (*Her eyes turn.*) Something's wrong, he must be hiding something from me! (*Her eyes turn again.*) He looked really nervous and he was in a hurry. As soon as he came through the door, he told me to go and get some water even before he took his clothes off. He seemed to be hiding something inside his gown. Let me search the place carefully!

[STORYTELLER *quietly sneaks up behind* CHANG E. *He beats the jar once again.*]

CHANG E	(*Turns around in shock.*) I don't know why, but I feel uneasy. I hope it's only my suspicious nature, but the whole thing still sends shivers down my spine. I could've sworn that an earthenware jar was standing here. He wouldn't let it out of his sight for one second even when he was drinking or making merry. But now it's nowhere to be found.

[STORYTELLER *again beats the jar once. He turns to one side and holds the jar in front of* CHANG E *in his outstretched hand, at the same time giving her a sidelong look.*]

CHANG E	So, it's here! Wait! How come it's facing this way? (*Takes the jar in her hand.*)

[*Exit* STORYTELLER *tiptoeing.*]

CHANG E	Nobody's allowed to come into the house. Who could've moved the jar except him? (*She looks around but sees no one.*)

[*Enter* WATCHMAN *carrying a wooden clapper. He beats the clapper.* CHANG E *is startled.*]

WATCHMAN	First watch. Close all doors and windows. Watch out for fire! (*Exit.*)

CHANG E	(*Looks at the jar.*) Where did this fruit come from? It's not a peach and it's not a plum. I wonder, did he go to the Queen Mother of the West and steal the no-death fruit? That was why he was in such a hurry, washing himself and going on a fast. I see it now: he wants to show respect to the gods, then he'll eat the fruit and leave me all alone. Poor Chang E, where's your lucky star? You've been driven out of Heaven, all on his account, and now he turns around and betrays you for another woman and eternal life. He doesn't care whether you're dead or alive. Oh Yi, you're so cruel!

[*Enter* WATCHMAN. *Beats the clapper twice.* CHANG E *is startled again.*]

WATCHMAN Second watch. Time for sleep. Beware of burglars! (*Exit.*)

CHANG E No wonder he has placed the entire house under heavy guard. His men are patrolling the grounds everywhere, both at the front and at the back. He also said that heads would roll should there be any mishaps. I see, he actually plans to leave me behind and return to Heaven alone under cover of darkness. I hate him. How can I ever forgive him? Now it's him or me! (*Swallows the no-death fruit.*)

[*Enter* WATCHMAN. *He beats the clapper three times.* CHANG E *walks around in circles with short and hurried steps.*]

WATCHMAN Third watch. All is secure. Sweet dreams. (*Exit.*)

CHANG E I can't stop wobbling. I feel light, as if I'm floating on air. Yi, oh Yi! Your wife has eaten the no-death fruit in a fit of anger, leaving none for you. What's to be done? What's to be done? I can't stop, I'm rising, taking flight. My good man, your wife doesn't want to leave you, but I can't … I'm powerless to resist the will of Heaven … (*Flies away and disappears.*)

[*Enter* WATCHMAN. *He stops and looks up at the sky.*]

WATCHMAN (*Beats his clapper continuously.*) Help! Help! Somebody, help!

[*Enter* CROWD *from all sides. They are running and carrying wooden sticks, swords and steel spears.*]

CROWD What the hell is going on?

	What's the racket about? Where's the criminal? What is it? A fire or a robbery?
WATCHMAN	Look! Quick, look at the sky!
CROWD	A monster? An evil spirit, it's flown to the moon! Yes, a toad! A bloody toad has climbed up onto the moon ...

[*Enter Y1 in a hurry. He stumbles upon the earthenware jar on the ground, picks it up and is stupefied.*]

WATCHMAN	(*Giggling.*) Sir, a big toad flew off to the moon.
YI	(*Throws away the jar and grips* WATCHMAN *by the throat with one hand.*) I'm gonna kill you, you son of a bitch!
WATCHMAN	(*Shaking all over.*) Sir ... please ... please forgive me ... (*Kneels.*)
YI	(*Lets go of* WATCHMAN, *looks up and laughs idiotically.*) For what it's worth, she's gone back to Heaven as she wanted, a big toad which will never die, ha ha ha ... (*Laughs madly.*) You people have always admired her for her beauty. How come you've become speechless all of a sudden? (*Silence.*) Heavenly Emperor, is this how you want to punish me? You could have proclaimed openly that Yi should be executed for killing the Sons of Heaven. That way, you'd have shown off your supreme power for all to see. Why then have you chosen to hide and punish me through a woman? A curse on you, Heavenly Emperor! A curse on you! (*Turns to* CROWD.) You people are so stupid you'll never understand. I saved you all for nothing. In the end I've only given away my own life. I hate myself as much as you do. Yi, what kind of hero do

	you think you are? Your many successes, the so-called immortal deeds, stink worse than a pile of dog shit!
	[WATCHMAN *stealthily picks up a wooden bat and gets to his feet. He gives* YI *a whack from behind.*]
YI	Alas.... A hero for nothing, rejected by Heaven, earth and men.... (*Falls to the ground.*)
	[CROWD *push forward and together they club* YI *to death.*
	Enter STORYTELLER *wearing a black headcloth and rolling a big wooden barrel. He beats the barrel continuously.*
	Enter WINGED DRAGON, WIND MASTER *and* RAIN CHIEF *fighting in earnest.* WINGED DRAGON *spits smoke and gas. He defeats* WIND MASTER *and* RAIN CHIEF, *who retreat.*
	Enter CHI YOU *hurriedly.*
STORYTELLER	(*Beats the barrel.*) Gods, spirits and demons, In Heaven and on earth, All fighting, all confused. This side, that side, They keep killing. Their spirits are high, all of them; Filled with moral anger, everyone. No rights or wrongs, Nor cause or effect. Show no pity, Show no mercy, For Heaven or for men. As long as there's fighting on stage, The audience'll go home happy. (*Exit rolling the wooden barrel.*)
WINGED DRAGON	Chi You, you're dead!

CHI YOU   My quarrel is with the Yellow Emperor. What's that got to do with you?

WINGED DRAGON   Let me show you what I've got! Winged Dragon is here to get you!

CHI YOU   Just a beast to ride on. Big Talk, capture this stupid reptile for me!

[*Enter BIG TALK, the giant, holding a peach wood staff. His hand is playing with the two yellow NINE-HEADED MONSTERS hanging down from his ears.*

BIG TALK   Here comes Big Talk. Watch what you're doing! (*Raises his staff and is about to club WINGED DRAGON with it.*) Take that!

[*Enter ARIDITY holding a big broom. With a sweep of her broom she approaches BIG TALK, and the sun penetrates the clouds and mists and shines glaringly in the sky.*

ARIDITY   (*Laughs madly.*) Ha ha ha, ha ha ha ha …

BIG TALK   (*Lifts his hands to cover his eyes.*) I can't see! My eyes, they're blind! It's the sun. I'm mad, really mad!

ARIDITY   (*Laughs madly.*) Ha ha ha, ha ha ha ha … (*Circles around BIG TALK.*)

[*Exit BIG TALK chasing after ARIDITY. Sunlight fades. All is enveloped in thick fog.*

Enter HEADLESS THE RECKLESS in pursuit of YELLOW EMPEROR, brandishing a broad axe in one hand and holding a shield in the other.

HEADLESS THE RECKLESS   It's you or me!

YELLOW EMPEROR   (*Yells in panic.*) Yu Hao, Yu Jing! Quick! Take out Thunder Beast's bone! Use it to beat the Giant Ox drum!

[*Enter Yu Hao and Yu Jing amidst fog and mist. They beat a huge drum. Thunder roars and lightning flashes. Enter Black Bear, Brown Bear, Tiger and Leopard, howling.*]

Winged Dragon Chi You, today you die!

Chi You (*Trembling uncontrollably when he hears Winged Dragon's words.*) Headless! Headless! Come quick! Lend me a hand!

[*Black Bear, Brown Bear, Tiger and Leopard fight with Headless, as Winged Dragon throws himself upon Chi You.*]

Chi You (*Gives a loud shriek, then dies.*) I'm doomed—

[*Headless turns as he hears Chi You's cry. Yellow Emperor wields his sword and chops off Headless' head, which Brown Bear picks up with his mouth, then runs away. Headless chases after Brown Bear. Exeunt.*]

Winged Dragon (*Getting carried away.*) Your Majesty! I finished Chi You with only one blow!

Yellow Emperor (*Still frightened. He approaches Chi You's body gingerly and scrutinizes it, pointing his sword at the body.*) Fasten heavy chains around the hands and feet of this thing. Expose the body in the great wilderness, so that it won't resurrect itself and cause endless trouble later on.

Yu Hao Yes, father.

[*Enter Black Bear and Brown Bear fighting for Headless the Reckless' head. Enter Headless brandishing his axe. His nipples have become his eyes and his belly button his mouth. He chases after Black Bear and Brown Bear.*]

Headless the Reckless (*Throws himself upon Black Bear and Brown Bear.*) Give me back my head!

[*Yellow Emperor is startled. Winged Dragon takes the*

	head from BLACK BEAR's *and* BROWN BEAR's *mouths and lifts it up high.*
WINGED DRAGON	Headless, Headless, over here. I've got it!
HEADLESS THE RECKLESS	(*Turns to attack* WINGED DRAGON.) Give me back my head!
WINGED DRAGON	(*Tosses the head back to* BLACK BEAR *and* BROWN BEAR.) That way, over there!
	[*All laugh. Only* YELLOW EMPEROR *is silent.*
HEADLESS THE RECKLESS	(*Despondent. Turns in circles.*) Give me back my head— Give me back my head—
WINGED DRAGON	(*Takes the head and plays with it with his feet. Teases* HEADLESS.) Look, down here. This way!
	[*All laugh again.* YELLOW EMPEROR *comes forward and stabs* HEADLESS *with his sword.* HEADLESS *falls to the ground and dies.*
YELLOW EMPEROR	Take his head and send it back to his hometown on Goat Mountain. Give it a stately funeral.
	[*All are shocked.*
YU HAO	Father, our people were valiant in battle and you still haven't bestowed their rewards on them yet. Aren't you being too generous to our enemy? With all due respect, I'm quite baffled.
YELLOW EMPEROR	He was loyal to his master to the very end. I admire his unflagging allegiance. (*Exit.*)
	[*Exit* YU HAO *holding* HEADLESS' *head in his hands. Also exeunt all hauling* CHI YOU's *and* HEADLESS' *bodies.*
	The hot sun is shining brightly. Enter BIG TALK *running and carrying a staff. He raises his staff and points it at the sun.*

BIG TALK   Cross the plains, climb the high mountains,
From East to West, roaming to Heaven's edge,
From morning till night, it's but one day,
Big Talk is my name.
I can run nonstop for three years. (*Leans on his staff and shields his eyes from the sun with his hand.*)
Cross ten thousand mountain ridges,
To the source of the Yellow River. (*Wobbling and in a swoon.*)
I easily drank all the water in the Yellow River;
I'm going to the River Wei to quench my thirst. (*Walks with difficulty while leaning on his staff.*)
Big Talk, are you going to die like this?
We'll see which one of us is the stronger … (*Panting continuously.*)
I'll leave you dozing on Yan Zi Mountain,
I'm heading north to find myself a big patch of water.
After I've quenched my thirst,
I'll storm your headquarters again … (*Looks ahead leaning on his staff.*)
Interminable sand dunes,
Endless dry land,
The setting sun is like blood,
And I'm dying of thirst— (*Wobbling.*)
Just an arm's length away— (*Raises his arm and points at the sun. Slowly sinks to the ground.*)
You're shaking all over, you're about to fall … (*Drops his arms. The staff is left standing erect.*)

[*Enter* STORYTELLER *quietly and empty-handed. He takes the staff in his hand.*]

STORYTELLER   (*Fiddles with the staff with his hand.*) In the days to come this abandoned staff will transform itself into a forest of peach trees stretching over a thousand miles. Admittedly there is yet another version of the story, which says that Big Talk did not die of thirst—he was actually killed by Winged Dragon. At any rate, when people get killed there must be killers, and when there are executioners there must be some people who are beheaded. Fighting a war is no different from playing cards: you win some and you lose some. The war between Flame Emperor and Yellow Emperor dragged on for a long time. In the end, Yellow Emperor sat unchallenged on his throne in the center of Heaven.

(*Suddenly a little bird pops out of his hand, as if by magic.*) Where did this come from? (*He stands the bird on the staff.*) Florid head, white beak and red claws. Lovely. (*Scrutinizing it.*) What? A pebble in her beak? (*Takes a pebble from the beak. Whistles and listens.*)

I see, your name is Jing Wei, and you want to fill up the East Sea with pebbles!
You say you didn't plan to do anything, you just wanted to play by the seaside.
Suddenly a hurricane appeared and evil waves surged up to the sky,
For no reason, all alone by yourself, you gave your life away!
Aren't you the spirit of Flame Emperor's lovely daughter Dolly?
The gods in Heaven were at war and this innocent little girl became the sacrificial lamb.
You say you're still young, you can't be a girl again, and you've no hope of love anymore.
What's the use of throwing pebbles into the sea one by one? How come you don't understand?
Oh, you say, no matter how big or how deep the sea, there's got to be a limit, but your regret will never end.
Little by little, day by day, and year by year, you're determined to fill up this vast and expansive sea!

Act II ▪ 73

[*Enter* LONG-LIFE HEMP *behind* STORYTELLER, *facing the audience.* STORYTELLER *immediately hides the little bird inside his clothes and turns.*

STORYTELLER   Another spirit comes uninvited.

[LONG-LIFE HEMP *turns. He has a white face and a big mouth. His eyes and his nose are one; there is no distinction.*

STORYTELLER   To whom do I owe the pleasure?

[LONG-LIFE HEMP *slowly opens his mouth, but no sound comes out.*

STORYTELLER   (*Approaches* LONG-LIFE HEMP.) I beg your pardon. Could you please tell me your name? Even a ghost has a name. You must be one of the gods.

[LONG-LIFE HEMP *opens his mouth wide and tries to shout. Still no sound comes out.*

STORYTELLER   I bet you don't have a tongue. Everybody says tongues can do a lot of harm. So it may not be a bad thing not to have a tongue, but you must have a voice, don't you? (*Silence.*) Then tell me, where did you come from? What are you in charge of? You look very dignified and imposing, you must be one of the honorable gods. Perhaps you could signal something with your hands.

[LONG-LIFE HEMP *points to a certain direction on the ground.*

STORYTELLER   The east?

[LONG-LIFE HEMP *half turns and points to another direction.*

STORYTELLER   The south?

[LONG-LIFE HEMP *turns again and points in a new direction.*

STORYTELLER   The north?

[LONG-LIFE HEMP *changes direction once more.*

STORYTELLER (*Walks around* LONG-LIFE HEMP *and looks at him.*) I see, you mean to say that you've got no shadow, is that it? You've got no sound and no shadow. Really amazing. I know, you wanted to say that you don't belong anywhere, you just wander all over the world, right? See, you're smiling. No sound, no shadow, no restraint. You must be a wonder spirit. Are you in charge of thinking? Or should I say you're as free as thinking and even the Heavenly Emperor himself can't restrain you? Maybe you're already free and easy and uncontrollable in the first place? Perhaps since you've no sound and no shadow, it makes no sense to talk about control—

[LONG-LIFE HEMP *disappears as the circle of light fades suddenly.*

STORYTELLER (*Suddenly understands.*) Of course, you're Long-Life Hemp! You come and go without a trace. (*Exit.*)

[*Curtain.*

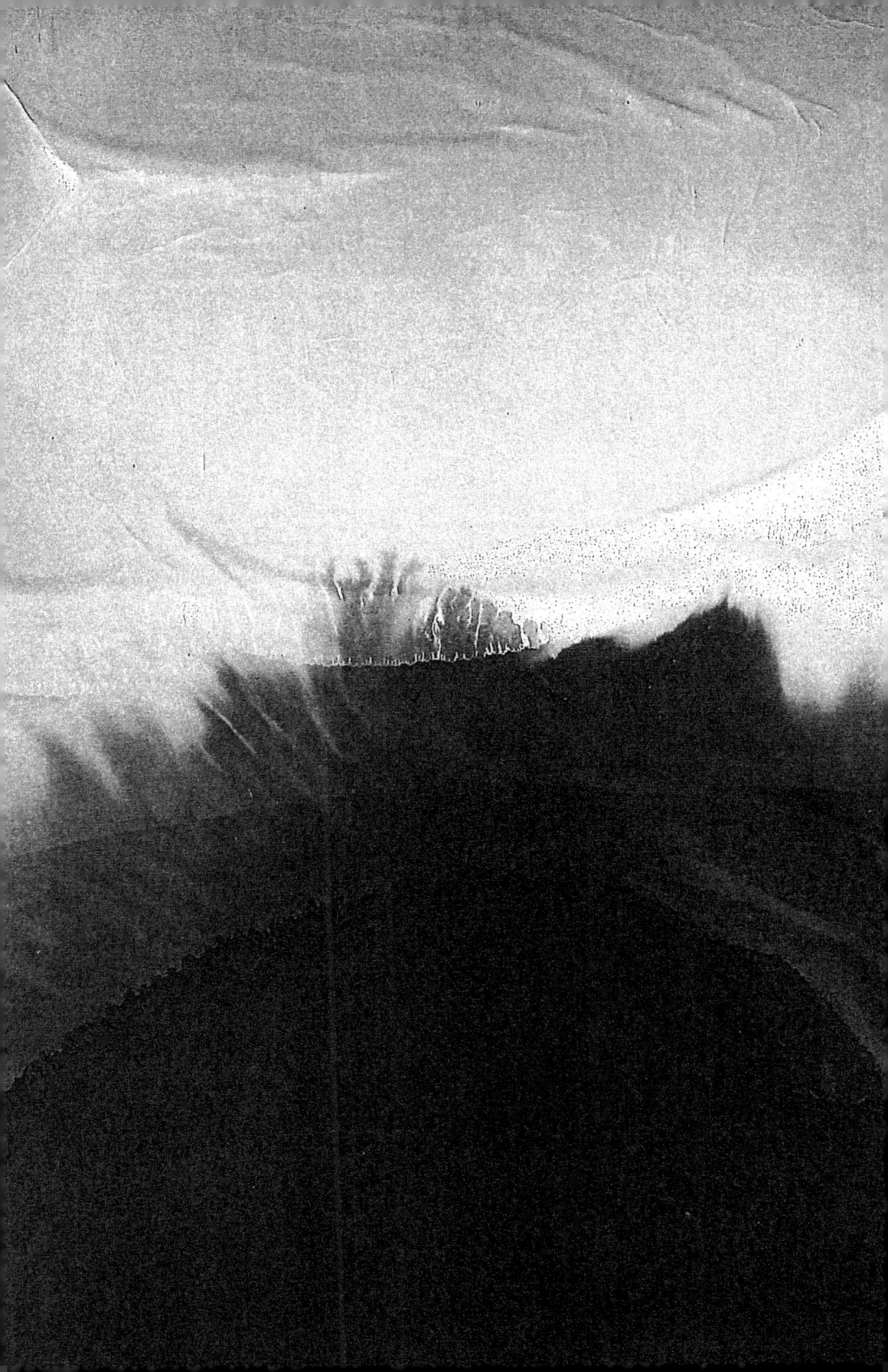

Act III

[*Heaven. The gods take their respective places. Tree God Gou Mang has a human face and the body of a bird. Fire God Zhu Rong is riding on two dragons. Shao Hao, descendant of the Yellow Emperor, has the head of an eagle and the body of a human. The Autumn God Ru Shou, also riding on two dragons, has a snake dangling from his left ear. Zhuan Xu, great grandson of the Yellow Emperor, has a long head, small ears, a human face, a pig's mouth and feet which are joined together. The Sea Spirits Yu Hao and Yu Jing. Earth God is made up as the king of Hades. The Giant Gods Chong and Li, who are brothers, both have painted faces and bare chests. Enter the Yellow Emperor. He sits high up in the Celestial Court.*]

YELLOW EMPEROR (*Proclaims solemnly.*) The entire universe is in chaos, because Heaven and earth are near to each other and the gods and the people live together in close proximity. When the gods fight one another, the people can't live in peace. From now on, traffic between Heaven and earth will be banned. People on earth should set down their rules for humans and the gods in Heaven must also keep to their order of things. The Able Emperor of Eastern Heaven has been playing with birds for so long that he has become confused. Now I command Fu Xi to be the Green Emperor. He may be old, but he is one of our forefathers, so I also command Tree God Gou Mang to render him assistance. Together they will govern Spring. The Flame Emperor of the Southern Heaven is becoming senile in his old age. His eyes and ears are not working well. He fails to manage his officials and subordinates, creating havoc in Heaven and on earth. I order Fire God Zhu Rong to take his place and govern Summer. The Queen Mother of the West thinks only about pursuing longevity and neglects her other duties. I order the God of Rosy Clouds, Shao Hao, to be the White Emperor. With assistance from his uncle, the God of Punishment Ru Shou, he will govern Autumn. As for the Northern Heaven, I order my great grandson Zhuan Xu to be the Black Emperor and my grandson Yu Jing to be his prime minister. Together they will govern Winter. And then there is the underworld of ghosts. I order Earth God, grandson of the Fire God, to be in charge of Death City. And I, the unrivaled and incomparable Heavenly Emperor, will position myself at the center of Heaven in the Celestial Court and keep a hold on the reigns of power over the four coigns.

[*All the gods bow.*]

YELLOW EMPEROR All my sons, grandsons and descendants, if you haven't been assigned any official duties, you will be sent down to earth to become kings or dukes, and be given your own land, officials, subjects, craftsmen and of course all kinds of entertainment. As Sons of Heaven and rulers of the people, you will, just as you do in Heaven, have your own cities, palaces, horse-drawn carriages, women and all kinds of musical instruments. There is only one exception. The pure sound of celestial music is prohibited on earth. Whoever contravenes the will of Heaven, whether he's a king, a ruler or a god, will be severely punished. Have I made myself clear?

[*All nod in agreement.*

YU HAO (*Takes one step forward.*) Your humble son has something to say, but he's not sure if he should say it.

YELLOW EMPEROR Let's hear it.

YU HAO Winged Dragon has devoted all his energy to putting down the rebellion. He has exhausted his magical powers and is no longer able to ascend to Heaven. In view of his meritorious deeds, would Your Majesty consider bestowing on him an appointment somewhere?

YELLOW EMPEROR That creature is restless and presumptuous. Send him to the South Pole.

YU HAO Your Majesty, how about sister? She's not well and she can't come up to Heaven either. She's now roaming aimlessly about on earth. Wherever she goes, there is heat and drought for a thousand miles, and all the crops fail. The people want to send her away but they don't dare.

YELLOW EMPEROR Send her to a place north of the Red River. No more roaming around.

YU HAO Yes, Your Majesty.

YELLOW EMPEROR And you, you'll still be the God of the Sea.... That's all.

YU HAO Yes, Your Majesty. (*Steps back.*)

YELLOW EMPEROR Black Emperor.

YU HAO (*Comes forward.*) Zhuan Xu, come forward and receive His Majesty's orders!

YELLOW EMPEROR	Cut off all roads between Heaven and earth. Play the Pure Sound of the Ox Horn.
ZHUAN XU	Yes, Your Majesty. Play the Pure Sound of the Ox Horn!
	[CHONG *and* LI *blow the horn. Exit the* YELLOW EMPEROR, *followed by others.*]
ZHUAN XU	Chong and Li, listen carefully!
LI	Tell us what it is you desire, grandpa.
ZHUAN XU	This is the Heavenly Emperor's decree.
CHONG	Your grandsons are listening.
ZHUAN XU	Cut off all roads between Heaven and earth at once. Leave only the Incomplete Mountain as the pillar to support Heaven. Allow no trespassers. Be on guard day and night. Make no mistakes! (*Exit.*)
LI	This isn't like blowing the ox horn. I've got no idea where to use my strength. Brother, I'm at my wit's end.
CHONG	(*Looking carefully up and down.*) Let me prop up Heaven with my hands. Then you push with your feet.
LI	It's not moving one bit, Brother!
CHONG	Wait till I count to three! One, two—
LI	Are you sure we can pry Heaven and earth apart like this? It'd have been so much easier if Nü Wa had separated them with her hands when she repaired the hole in Heaven.
CHONG	Stop moaning. Take a deep breath and hold it!
LI	I'm holding it—
CHONG	Breathe in really deep before holding it! Wait till I count to three—

Li	If we don't do this properly and the sky collapses, we'll both be flattened like pancakes.
Chong	The sky is propped up by a celestial column. What're you afraid of? Listen to my count: one, two, three—

[*The sky rises and the earth sinks. In between emerges the celestial column, that is, Incomplete Mountain.*

Enter Gong Gong *in a hurry. He has red hair, a human face and a snake's body.*

Li	Yo! Where do you think you're going?
Gong Gong	Heaven.
Li	What for?
Gong Gong	To settle a score.
Li	Where did this bastard come from? He's got a big mouth, that's for sure!
Chong	Get his name.
Gong Gong	Gong Gong is the name.
Chong	(*Checking him over.*) By His Majesty's decree, no one is allowed to go up to Heaven.
Gong Gong	Which His Majesty?
Chong	His Majesty the Black Emperor, our grandfather.
Gong Gong	That black swine? You call him His Majesty? Surely you jest.
Li	Have you got a death wish?
Gong Gong	Look kid, watch what you're saying. Just tell that black swine to come out.
Chong	I'd tread carefully if I were you. If you wanna be king, go back to your Gong Gong country in the south.

GONG GONG	Your uncle Gong Gong here needs to go up to Heaven to reason with that black swine.
LI	Reason? You think you've got the brains to do that?
CHONG	(*Pulls Li away.*) Reasoning with people depends not on force but on the volume of one's voice. So just go ahead and shout, and see if His Majesty will answer you.
GONG GONG	(*Yells.*) Zhuan Xu, Zhuan Xu! You stupid swine!
CHONG	(*Stops Li.*) Don't be so rude or you'll end up like that idiot Yi. We can't be held responsible.
GONG GONG	Come down if you have any guts. Only cowards pretend to be deaf and dumb. You stupid black swine, I'm curious to know how you're managing as emperor. (*Exit, running toward the celestial column.*)

[*Sound of Heaven and earth cracking. Enter* STORYTELLER *in a hurry, half of his face painted. He is holding a paintbrush in his hand.*]

STORYTELLER	What is it now? Heaven has just become a peaceful place, but there's still unrest on earth. The problem is, everybody wants to be God. But if everybody becomes God, God will be no more. And if everybody goes up to Heaven, how will there be any people left on earth? If everybody becomes the boss, who are they going to boss around? Ladies and gentlemen, if everybody came here to watch our play like you, there wouldn't be so many troubles in the world, would there? (*Exit.*)

[*Heaven and earth split apart.*

CHONG	What's this guy doing?
LI	He's smashing the celestial column, Incomplete Mountain, with his head.

CHONG   Oh no, the sky and the stars are tilting toward the west.

LI   The earth has split open. The southeast has sunk into the sea!

CHONG   Quick! Go and report to His Majesty!

           [*Severe flooding. Cries for help everywhere. Enter GUN.*]

GUN   All the land, all the fields have been engulfed in water. The houses are all gone. People are living like fish and sea turtles. There's water everywhere. I'm anxious, and my heart is sick with worry. Your Majesty, you ordered me to administer this land, but given the circumstances, how can I do my job well? We're all your offspring, so why have you treated us differently? I know my place, but forgive me if I venture to say a few words. As the supreme ruler of Heaven, you can't just ignore the cries for help coming from all over the earth. You say that you don't want to be bothered, and you don't want to look after the affairs on earth, its people and officials, anymore. But just tell me what to do, even if it's only a hint. I'll do things according to Your Majesty's wishes. Your Majesty, do you hear my prayer?

           [*Enter CHI OWL and TORTOISE slowly, each holding one end of a piece of grass in its mouth. They are dragging and pulling at each other.*]

GUN   This is water country; only owls and tortoises can get by and survive.

CHI OWL   My!

GUN   Who goes there?

CHI OWL   My!

GUN   (*Looks around.*) Not a soul anywhere. Doom and gloom all over the place.

TORTOISE	Don't despair.
GUN	(*Lowers his head.*) Isn't that Chi Owl and Tortoise talking?
TORTOISE	Yes. Don't be sad.
GUN	How could you, an owl and a tortoise, understand my anxieties? Heaven has given me this land to govern. It's given me officials and people as well. But look at me now, I'm the only one left, how can my heart not be sick with worry?
TORTOISE	If I remember correctly, the Yellow Emperor fathered Luo Ming, and Luo Ming fathered White Horse. White Horse is you, Gun. Am I right?
GUN	Yes.
CHI OWL	My! Then you're a direct descendant of the Heavenly Emperor himself!
GUN	You don't understand. I may be the Yellow Emperor's eldest grandson, but I hardly ever get the chance to see him.
CHI OWL	He's your grandfather no matter what. He has to do something if his grandson's in trouble, hasn't he? My! My!
GUN	(*Sighs.*) It's no use praying or pleading with him. If I go and bother him again, I'll only make him even angrier.
TORTOISE	If I remember correctly … I only heard this from the old folks…. There's something called Ever-growing Soil in Heaven. It never stops growing. If you use some of it, it grows back again.
GUN	Now that you mention it, it's all over the place in the Heavenly Garden … but I wonder how I'm going to lay my hands on some of that magical soil?

CHI OWL	You're the Heavenly Emperor's eldest grandson. How could anyone stop you? Just go and grab some with your hands.
GUN	That's not a bad idea … but if the Heavenly Emperor gets wind of this, I'll be in deep trouble!
CHI OWL	My! He's given you the earth, what's a handful of Ever-growing Soil? My!
GUN	It's true he's given me the earth, but he didn't give me the Ever-growing Soil.
TORTOISE	But there hasn't been any flood in Heaven. I didn't hear our ancestors say anything about it, if I remember correctly.
CHI OWL	It's a test the Heavenly Emperor's given you. He wants you to be king and he's seeing if you're able to do the job.
GUN	You've got a point there! (*Exit.*)

[Both CHI OWL and TORTOISE *are pulling at the same blade of grass with their mouths. In the end both fall into the water.*

Enter STORYTELLER. *The right side of his face is painted in color and the left side is covered with a half-mask.*

STORYTELLER	Ladies and gentlemen, please take a guess. Guess what kind of monster this is. (*Turns to show the left side of his face, revealing a horrifying tiger's head.*) Doesn't this look like a tiger? (*Turns to show the right side of his face, which is that of a clown.*) When people fight, it picks up the good guys in its mouth and carries them away. As for the bad guys, who're usually cruel and unreasonable, it brings them all kinds of birds and animals in its mouth. And if it realizes that you're honest, it'll bite off your nose in one go! This monster is called Weird Beast Qiong Qi. (*Exit.*)

[*Gun walks briskly, his head lowered.*

Voice from the Sky   Gun—

[Gun *halts immediately. He raises his head to listen. Hearing no sound, he starts to stroll along slowly as if nothing has happened.*

Voice from the Sky   Gun!

[Gun *halts again. He looks around in confusion, turns and runs. Enter* Fire God Zhu Rong *holding a sword. He stops* Gun.

Fire God   Didn't you hear the voice of the Heavenly Emperor?

Gun   Yes, I did.

Fire God   If you heard him, then why didn't you put it down?

Gun   Put what down?

Fire God   What you're holding in your hand.

Gun   I didn't take anything. (*Holds out his right hand.*) I don't need to—

Fire God   Open your left hand.

Gun   (*Opens left hand.*) I'm no thief. I've got everything on earth.

Fire God   Both hands! Open both hands for me!

Gun   (*Opens both hands.*) I've come here to relax. The earth is being devastated by a big flood and I'm fed up.

Fire God   Lift your thumb! What's this?

Gun   Just a piece of Ever-growing Soil. I just took a tiny bit in passing, as a souvenir.

Fire God   Don't you know that the earth is prohibited from having anything that's to be found in Heaven?

GUN	Fire God, aren't you the eldest grandson of the Black Emperor? Don't you recognize me? Your grandfather is my junior—
FIRE GOD	I said, put down the Ever-growing Soil!
GUN	I'm the eldest grandson of the Heavenly Emperor! Don't talk to me like that!
FIRE GOD	I'm under the Heavenly Emperor's orders to protect this place. I have a job to do.
GUN	Take a good look down there. The earth is covered with flood water. It's become an ocean. Only Ever-growing Soil can stop the water now. You're one of the gods and you have a duty to assist the Heavenly Emperor to make the earth a peaceful place to live in.
FIRE GOD	I've got no time to argue with you. Do as I told you. Put the Ever-growing Soil down!

[GUN *is about to make a run for it.*]

FIRE GOD	(*Takes out his sword and confronts* GUN.) Are you going to put it down or not?
GUN	(*Very annoyed.*) How could you? I'm not a commoner, a man in the street! If the Heavenly God knew about this, he wouldn't just do nothing and abandon his subjects. How long have you been serving the Heavenly Emperor, sonny?
FIRE GOD	(*Strikes* GUN *with his sword.*) Take that!
GUN	Oh— (*Shocked. His mouth wide open, he staggers to one side and falls.*)
FIRE GOD	(*Wipes his sword.*) I'm only carrying out the Heavenly Emperor's orders. (*Takes the Ever-growing Soil from* GUN's *hand. Exit.*)

[*Gun, wobbling along, runs for a short distance and arrives at the gate of Death City on Feather Mountain.*

There is ice and snow everywhere. Neither the sun nor the moon can be seen. In the darkness, Torch Dragon is crouching. It has a human face, a dragon's head, a scarlet snake's body and a pair of huge eyes which keep opening and shutting. It guards the front gate day and night.

Gun finally collapses outside the gate of Death City.

Enter Shen Tu and Yu Lei carrying peach wood sticks. Both of them are naked from the waist up. Their heads are bald and have horns growing on them.

Shen Tu	Another dead one.
Yu Lei	Are you on duty or am I on duty?
Shen Tu	Yu Lei, when you were on duty, did I get any rest? This guy is really heavy. Come and give me a hand.
Yu Lei	Look! The eyes are still open!
Shen Tu	Why don't you close them?
Yu Lei	What the hell? I closed them once and they're open again.
Shen Tu	Harder! Press harder! Press the eyelids together!
Yu Lei	Slow down. We can't drag any living person into Death City. There are rules we have to follow in this job.
Shen Tu	He's not breathing, right?
Yu Lei	Let me ask you a question: how do you declare somebody dead?
Shen Tu	(*Reciting regulations.*) No breath coming from either the nose or mouth—and eyelids closed or—unable to open or remaining closed after handling, only in such cases—

Yu Lei	Case closed. We can't just take people in at random. This is Death City, not unjust city. We only take in dead people, those who're really dead. That's how we've been operating for a long, long time. When did you see your old buddy Yu Lei here make a mistake?
Shen Tu	Have you quite finished? Since you've been doing all the talking, why don't you tell me what we're gonna do? We can't just leave him lying here blocking the entrance to the gate. If our boss sees him, he'll say that it ruins the view of Death City or something.
Yu Lei	(*Examines Gun closely.*) Goodness! Isn't he Gun, ruler of the earth and eldest grandson of the Heavenly Emperor?
Shen Tu	Shall we carry him back to earth right now?
Yu Lei	Maybe their family is having a fight among themselves. We shouldn't take sides. Don't rush into doing anything. Let's go and ask the Earth God!

[*Exit Shen Tu.*]

Yu Lei	(*Circling Gun.*) Whatever grievances you may have, Lord Gun, please be frank and tell me about them. If you don't have any, then just close your eyes and die in peace. I'm not afraid of anything. I've seen my share of dead people and ghosts. I'm not bragging, but I eat thirty thousand ghosts for breakfast and another three thousand for midnight snack. Whatever's left, I tie them all up with a piece of straw, drag them away and feed them to the tigers. I'm a professional ghost-eater. Since I'm a professional, why should I fear ghosts, even if they won't rest easy when they die? I just hope that someone like you, who may or may not be a ghost, won't break my valuable rice bowl and get me fired from my job.

[*Enter Shen Tu.*]

YU LEI	What did he say?
SHEN TU	The Earth God went to report to the Heavenly Emperor. He didn't dare make a decision himself.
YU LEI	Lucky for us. Didn't I tell you that that guy's no small fry?

[*Enter* WU THE KNIFE, *one of the Heavenly Gods.*]

WU	Where's Gun, that shameless bastard who refuses to die?
SHEN TU	Where? He's lying across the gate to Death City.
YU LEI	Stop! Who goes there? Who dares to brandish a knife at us?
WU THE KNIFE	I'm Heavenly God Wu the Knife. I'm here on the orders of His Majesty the Heavenly Emperor! (*Cuts open* GUN'S *belly with his knife.*)

[*The stage suddenly turns dark. A yellow bear raises its head and howls.*]

YU LEI	Goodness, a bear's wriggling out of the belly!

[SHEN TU *and* YU LEI *flee. Exeunt.*

Yu is born, breaking open the bear's skin from inside the bear.

WU	Yu, prostrate yourself and receive His Majesty's decree!

[*Yu prostrates himself.*

VOICE FROM THE SKY	Your father dedicated his life to overcoming the flood even unto his death. In commemoration of his devotion, His Majesty has commanded me to provide you with some Ever-growing Soil. He has also instructed Winged Dragon to help you open up the roads. Your responsibilities are heavy. Make no mistakes.

Yu	The orders have come from Heaven. Yu would not dare to be remiss in carrying out his duties.
	[Wu the Knife *gives some Ever-growing Soil and a precious sword to* Yu. *Exit.*
Voice from the Sky	When calm returns to earth, you will become king. With the power vested in you, you will maintain law and order.
Yu	(*Kowtows.*) Yu remains forever grateful for His Majesty's favors, which he'll never forget. (*Stands up and looks into the distance. Exit.*)
	[*The sky gradually brightens. A high platform emerges on one side of the stage.* Aide Willow (Xiang Liu), *who has a human face and a snake's body, curls up on top of the platform.*
	Enter Yu. *He is wearing a sword and is holding some Ever-growing Soil in his hand wrapped in a piece of cloth.*
	Enter Storyteller, *wearing a clown's costume. He is waving two colored sticks, on which are hung copper coins. The coins clank loudly.*
Yu	Demons, evil spirits and monsters, listen carefully. Yu has received his mandate from Heaven. All those who are respectful and acquiescent will be given official titles and awards, and all those who give rise to discord or unrest will be executed!
Aide Willow	I, Aide Willow, am an officer in Gong Gong's service. My duty is to guard the ancestral ceremonial altar. I don't take orders from the Heavenly Emperor, let alone a bastard fathered by a bear, a baby still sucking milk from his mother's breast.
Yu	How many heads have you got, gutter mouth? (*Raises his sword and gets ready to chop.*)

AIDE WILLOW   (*Sticks out another head from behind* YU.) Don't you know that I, Aide Willow, (*Sticks out another head.*) I, Aide Willow, (*Sticks out yet another head.*) I, Aide Willow, I, Aide Willow, I, Aide Willow, I, Aide Willow, I, Aide Willow, I, Aide Willow, (*Sticks out nine heads altogether.*) have nine heads—

[YU *fights a ferocious battle with* AIDE WILLOW *the nine-headed monster, but soon his strength begins to fail. In his anxiety, he has an idea—he scatters the Ever-growing Soil in the air, blinding* AIDE WILLOW. *As* YU *leaps up onto the altar, all of* AIDE WILLOW'S *nine heads recoil in horror underneath.*]

AIDE WILLOW   Don't defile the sacred altar! You, come down at once! Don't you have any ancestors yourself? Come down! Come down! Don't you have parents? Come down! Come down! Come down now! Don't you have any taboos? Any fears? Come down! Come down! And no faith? No inhibitions at all? Come down at once!

YU   I have a father but no mother; I have guts but no fear; I have balls and no cold feet; I have support and I don't scare easily. I stand alone, I don't need anybody. My only goal is to assist the Heavenly Emperor! (*Laughs loudly.*) Take that, you bonehead!

[AIDE WILLOW'S *nine heads crawl on the ground wailing. Each time* YU *cuts off a head, he covers the blood with a handful of Ever-growing Soil. Then he stands up straight and looks around.* STORYTELLER *waves his stick with more and more vigor as he moves among the heads.*]

STORYTELLER   (*Sings and recites.*)
Yu fights on, making conquests here and there,
A real big hero of his time and day.
In the north he conquers Stone Mountain,
With Winged Dragon opening the way.

In the south he overcomes Gong Gong's state,
In the west to Mount Cloudy he makes a foray.

Everywhere he goes, the Ever-growing Soil he strews,
Until he comes to the East Sea shore,
The country of Mountain Blue.
He sees the nine-tailed fox,
It looks auspicious and true.

And then at the foot of Mountain Tu,
He sees a beautiful young maid.
She walks with clear clinking sounds,
On her body she wears rings of jade.
Yu may be half-beast and half-god,
But love and romance he cannot evade.

[*Enter* PRETTY MAID, *demure and deeply in love. Enter* YU *limping. He takes* PRETTY MAID *by the hand. Exeunt.*

STORYTELLER (*Reciting while dancing. Changing his routine at times.*)
So a Son of Heaven makes love with a maiden from earth.
And surprise, surprise!
He suddenly reveals his true identity—
A big yellow bear!

[*Enter* PRETTY MAID *running, a yellow bear chasing close behind her.*

STORYTELLER (*Switches to spoken dialog.*)
So horrified is the young maiden,
Who quickly turns into a stone.
The anxious Yu commands the stone, "Open! Open!"
Thus "Open" becomes the name of his son. (*Suddenly stops.*)

[*The yellow bear takes the baby from* PRETTY MAID's *arms with its mouth. Exit.*

PRETTY MAID *is extremely embarrassed. Exit.*

STORYTELLER   Members of the audience, the last scene actually happens later. I was carried away and got ahead of myself. Now let's get back to our play.

[STORYTELLER *retires to one side.*

Enter dukes and princes from all sides.

STORYTELLER   (*Recites.*)
His dreams realized,
His nation-building done,
Yu orders, in commemoration,
The forging of nine bronze tripods.
Dukes and princes from all points,
Assemble atop the mountain at Hui Ji,
They wait, in deference, for the Emperor
To bestow on them their rewards.

[*Enter* YU *escorted by* WINGED DRAGON *and guards.*

WINGED DRAGON   Let the coronation of His Majesty Emperor Yu commence!

[*Instantly there is music and a drum roll. Enter* WINDSHIELD *the giant, shabbily dressed, with a leather string around his waist and shoes made of hemp. The gods talk among themselves.*

WINGED DRAGON   Windshield, the Homage to Heaven Ceremony was scheduled for noon. Why have you come so late?

WINDSHIELD   I'm here, aren't I? On any other day I would only just have got up at this hour. (*Giggles.*)

[*All snigger.*

YU   (*Calmly, without showing emotion.*) Take him away. Decapitate him.

[*Guards left and right come forward and take hold of* WINDSHIELD. WINGED DRAGON *raises his sword.*

WINDSHIELD	No! Please don't! Please don't! (*Howls.*) It's not fair! Your Majesty—It's not fair …
	[*All are silent. Loud music and drum roll. Enter the pygmy* HIKER SHU HAI. *He takes a small ruler about seven inches long from under* YU's *seat.*
STORYTELLER	(*Spoken dialog.*) So Yu orders his courtier Hiker to take measurements of the land.
	[HIKER *runs in small steps from left to right to take measurements, counting at the same time.*
YU	How far is it from the easternmost end to the westernmost end?
HIKER	Five hundred million and seven *xuan*, eight *xuan*, nine *xuan*, ten *xuan*—(*Passes by the side of* STORYTELLER.)
STORYTELLER	(*Bends down.*) Pardon me, may I ask how long is one *xuan*?
HIKER	(*Gives* STORYTELLER *a look of annoyance.*) One *xuan* is equal to ten thousand.
STORYTELLER	Members of the audience, this Yu doesn't leave anything to chance. The earth may be big, but he wants to know exactly how big it is.
HIKER	(*Stands on tiptoe and reports to* YU *in a loud voice.*) Your Majesty, the measurement of the earth is: five hundred million, one hundred and nine thousand, eight hundred paces!
	[YU *stands up and limps along. He clasps his palms together to pay homage to Heaven. All chant in response.*
STORYTELLER	(*Picks up his stick and starts to tap continuously, giving his all.*) This is the end of the mythological age, From now on, it'll be the age of history,

Of princes, emperors and kings.
Farmers quietly farm their land,
Matchmakers make their matches,
And boat trackers tow their boats.
As for scholars, it's very hard to say:
Either they write to show off their literary knack,
Or they climb the official ladder,
Taking up high positions with handsome pay.
Only the common bean curd sellers are suffering.
They toss and turn in their beds every night,
Wracking their brains a thousand times.
But they just can't figure it out,
They still have to sell their bean curds,
Come the morning of the next day.

The first draft was completed in the early morning of February 13, 1989 in Paris.

Revised on January 26, 1993.

On Performing
Of Mountains and Seas

Gao Xingjian

1. *Of Mountains and Seas* is based on the early myths as recorded in the ancient text *The Classic of Mountains and Seas*. Every effort has been made to remove the interpretations added onto the text by later scholars. The plot of the play is made up of the major stories of the gods, and in this I have tried to be as faithful to the original as possible. Thus the Chinese title describes the play as a "biography" (*zhuan* 傳) and not an "adaptation" (*xinbian* 新編).

2. Quite a few scholars have conducted research on this classic text, including Lu Xun 魯迅, Wen Yiduo 聞一多 and our contemporary Yuan Ke 袁珂. Our play has especially relied upon Yuan Ke's research and studies. Without his work, it would have taken me a much longer time to complete the play, for then I would have to sift through the voluminous books on the subject.

3. Ancient Chinese mythology is no less rich and colorful than Greek mythology. Unfortunately, it has been cut and altered by generations of orthodox Confucianists, who have rendered it unrecognizable; they almost managed to bury its true look and characteristics. I have tried to restore the innocence in ancient Chinese mythology, which I consider richer than any kind of rationalized interpretations of the text.

4. Our play is a return to the dramatic tradition of ancient China. I suggest that the performance should adopt the form of a variety show, borrowing elements from the styles of the roadside salesman, the medicine man, monkey shows, acrobatics, puppetry and shadow plays,

and the candy man. The atmosphere can be likened to the hustle and bustle in a temple fair. Of course, other methods are also possible and should not be ruled out.

5. The make-up and acting of the gods in the play may find inspiration from all kinds of Chinese folk art forms. They may wear masks, painted faces and plumed headgear; they may engage in acrobatics, sword play and other martial arts; they may put on stilts, wooden clogs, ride on paper ponies and carry dragon lanterns; and they may perform somersaults, wire-walking and stilt tricks. That is, if the actors have had the necessary training. Of course, new and unconventional tricks can also be introduced. If they are popular, make them as popular as possible; if they are clownish, make them as clownish as possible. Both falsetto and real voice can be used; winking and making faces are allowed; and crying and laughing do not have to be real.

6. The Storyteller's make-up, costume, and singing and reciting can be guided by the ancestral worship ceremony of the Miao people, the chanting of the sutra of the Yi people, the folk singing in Jingzhou and the singing-talking love songs of the Lixia River in northern Jiangsu. These performances, combining dialog with singing, are sometimes conducted in high pitch, and at other times they are carried out in low and deep tones. They can be comical, but they can also pretend to be serious with a hint of make-believe.

7. As for set design and the appearance of the gods, one can refer to the bronze vessels of the Shang dynasty (especially the statues and ceremonial vessels recently excavated from Sichuan), the lacquer wares excavated from the Chu tombs, the silk paintings and stone and brick carvings of the Han dynasty, and the rock painting found in Yunnan and Guangxi provinces. Never fall into the trap of imitating the vulgarity of the popular art which emerged after the Tang and Song dynasties both inside and outside the imperial court.

Notes

Able Emperor	Di Jun 帝俊. The Able Emperor was the god worshiped by the Yin 殷 people, who later founded the Shang 商 dynasty. The myths associated with the Able Emperor are quite fragmented. It is said that he has two wives: Sun Mother Xi He 羲和, who gives birth to ten suns, and Moon Mother Chang Yi 常儀, who gives birth to twelve moons. He also has another wife by the name of E Huang 娥皇 in the south; she begets a child who has three bodies. The Able Emperor always comes down from Heaven and socializes with the dancing Five-Colored Birds. He owns a bamboo forest. It is possible to cut off a section of the bamboo trees there to make a boat.
Aide Willow	Xiang Liu 相柳. Aide Willow is Gong Gong's 共工 minister. He has the body of a green snake. He likes violence and has an insatiable appetite for food, thus he has nine heads with human faces so that he can consume the food on all the nine mountains at the same time. All the places he touches become ravines and swamps. When Yu 禹 kills him, his blood makes the soil smell so bad that no crops can be planted. Yu has to dig up the soil to a depth of three *ren* (24 feet) and cleanse it three times. Some of the soil is used to make a mound tower to pay homage to all the emperors.

Aridity	Ba 魃. Daughter of the Yellow Emperor 黃帝. She always appears in green clothes. During the war against Chi You, the Yellow Emperor sends her down from Heaven to stop the rainstorm conjured up by Chi You's helpers Wind Master and Rain Chief. After such a fierce battle, she has used up all her power and is too weak to ascend back to Heaven. So she roams around on earth, causing droughts wherever she goes. The Yellow Emperor therefore orders her to stay at a place north of the Red River 赤水, but she frequently wanders to other areas.
Autumn God	Ru Shou 蓐收. He lives in the West and rides on two dragons. There is a snake attached to his left ear.

In the play, Ru Shou is also referred to as the God of Punishment. |
Ba 魃	See Aridity.
Bi Li 萆荔	A fragrant creeper which grows on rocks and tree trunks, eaten to cure heart pain.
Big People Country	Daren Guo 大人國. A country of big people. They sit and row their boats. There is a marketplace on the mountain called the Big People Hall, on top of which kneels a big man, with his arms stretched out wide.
Big Pig	Feng Xi 封豨. A fabled animal with sharp teeth and claws. More powerful than a bull, it damages crops and feeds on human beings and domestic animals.
Big Talk	Kua Fu 夸父. Big Talk wears two yellow snakes as ear ornaments and holds two yellow snakes in his hands.

His strength knows no bounds and he wants to chase the sun. He catches up with it at Ape Valley 禺谷. By sunset, he has run a long way, so he drinks the water from the Yellow River 黃河 and the Wei River 渭水. The water in these rivers proves insufficient to quench |

his thirst, so he travels north, hoping to drink from the Big Marsh 大澤, which is one thousand *li* wide, but he dies of thirst before he reaches it. The walking staff he abandons turns into a forest, which provides shade for the people.

Big Talk is regarded as presumptuous because he refuses to admit his limitations. Some recent scholars praise Big Talk for his romanticism; others laud him because he attempts to conquer nature.

Big Wind Peacock	Da Feng 大風. Wherever Big Wind Peacock flies it stirs up a gale, hence its name.
Bright Beast	Kai Ming Shou 開明獸. The Bright Beast has a huge body and looks like a tiger with nine human heads. The nine gates on the Kun Lun 崑崙 Mountains are each guarded by a Bright Beast.
Bu Zhou Zhi Shan 不周之山	See Incomplete Mountain.
Chang E 嫦娥	Yi's 羿 wife. She steals the elixir of immortality from her husband, gulps it down and flies to the moon. She is regarded as the moon goddess and icon of the Mid-autumn Festival.
Chang Yi 常儀	See Moon Mother.
Chi Owl	Chi 鴟. An owl-like bird with one head and three bodies.
Chi You 蚩尤	Chi You is a tribal chief, an inventor of weapons and a divine being who challenges the rule of the Yellow Emperor. In the famous Battle of Zhuo Lu 涿鹿之戰 that ensues, the Yellow Emperor orders Winged Dragon 應龍 to attack Chi You. When Winged Dragon uses the water he has been hoarding to attack Chi You's army, Chi You asks Wind Master 風師 and Rain Chief 雨伯 to create a huge rainstorm to counterattack.

Finally, the Yellow Emperor has to send for his daughter Aridity to come down from Heaven, and she succeeds in overcoming Wind Master and Rain Chief with her scorching sunshine.

Another legend has it that during his battle with the Yellow Emperor, Chi You creates a great fog which lasts three days to disorient his enemies. The resourceful Yellow Emperor then invents chariots equipped with a compass, and his soldiers are able to find the directions. After many fierce battles, he finally defeats and kills Chi You.

The battle is one between brains and brawn. The Yellow Emperor, the consummate strategist, is the victor and has been revered as a wise king and the forefather of the Chinese race. The loser Chi You, though brave and strong, has been regarded as the villain in Chinese mythology, and his acts of strength and bravery have been condemned as ruthless and insidious.

Chiseled Teeth	Zao Chi 鑿齒. A manlike monster with fangs five or six feet long. It terrorizes people and is killed by Yi the Archer.
Chong and Li 重、黎	Chong is an official in charge of wood (trees) and Li is in charge of fire. Later, Chong is appointed an officer of the south for monitoring the sky and Li oversees the north and manages the people's affairs on earth. The Heavenly Emperor orders the two to erect a barrier between Heaven and earth, so that the realms of the gods and the people are separate and no traffic between them is allowed.
Da Feng 大風	See Big Wind Peacock.
Daren Guo 大人國	See Big People Country.

Death City	You Du 幽都. A mountain in the North Sea 北海; also the source of the Black River 黑水. On the mountain there are black birds, black snakes, black panthers, black tigers and black foxes with bushy tails.
Di Jun 帝俊	See Able Emperor.
Dolly	Nü Wa 女娃. The story goes that Dolly, the younger daughter of the Flame Emperor 炎帝, goes for a swim in the East Sea and is drowned. Then she turns into a bird called Jing Wei 精衛, a divine bird which looks like a crow, with a striped head, a white beak and red feet. Its call sounds like its name. For eternity the bird carries twigs and pebbles from the Western Mountains 西山 in her beak in an attempt to fill up the vast East Sea. She is regarded as a symbol of perseverance.
Earth God	Hou Tu 后土. Grandson of the Fire God. He is appointed by the Yellow Emperor to administer Death City.
Emperor Yan 炎帝	See Flame Emperor.
Ever-growing Soil	Xi Rang 息壤. Soil that keeps expanding once it touches the earth. Gun 鯀 tries to steal it from Heaven and use it to control the flood.
Fang Feng Shi 防風氏	See Windshield.
Feather Mountain	Yu Mountain 羽山. On this mountain, rainfall is heavy high up and water is plentiful at the foot, but vegetation is scarce. There are many cobras there. Gun 鯀, Yu's 禹 father, is executed on Feather Mountain.
Feng Huang Luan Niao 鳳凰鸞鳥	See Phoenixes and Wonder Birds.
Feng Xi 封豨	See Big Pig.
Fire God	Zhu Rong 祝融. The Fire God has the body of an animal and a human face, and rides on two dragons.

Five-Colored Birds	Wu Cai Niao 五采鳥. The five colors referred to are yellow, green, white, red, and black. Five-Colored Birds frequently flutter their wings and dance with one another. They are friends with the Able Emperor and oversee his two altars under the sky at the foot of his mountain.
Flame Emperor	Yan Di 炎帝. Also known as Shen Nong 神農 (God of Agriculture). The emperor of South Heaven. He has a human body and a cow's head.
	It is said that a red bird carrying a stalk full of grain in its mouth flies across the sky and drops the grains onto the ground. The Flame Emperor picks them up, plants them in the field, and they grow tall and big. People eat them to alleviate their hunger and they live forever. The Flame Emperor has also invented various farming tools, taught people how to farm, weave and raise cattle, make pottery and use fire (thus his name *yan* 炎, meaning fire).
	The Flame Emperor is also the God of Medicine. It is said that he has a transparent body which shows his internal organs such as lungs, liver and so on. He tastes all kinds of herbs to test their medicinal properties. Because of this, he was once poisoned twelve times in a day, but each time he was able to save himself with an antidote (or because he has a transparent body, he can see where the poison has gone).
	There are also accounts of the Flame Emperor's battle with the Yellow Emperor, in which the Flame Emperor's weapon of fire is overcome by the Yellow Emperor's use of water, so that the battle for the possession of the whole cosmos is won by the latter. Some ancient texts say that the two heavenly emperors are brothers.

Fu Fei 宓妃	The beautiful daughter of the god Fu Xi 伏羲. She is drowned in the Luo River 洛水 and becomes the Goddess of the Luo River. Later she marries the River Lord.
Gentlemen Country	Junzi Guo 君子國. People in this country are well dressed and wear swords. They are polite and avoid getting into quarrels. They eat animals and train two large tigers to stay by their sides.
Giant Ox	Kui Niu 夔牛. A mythological animal shaped like a cow, with a deep green body, no horns and one foot. When it goes into and emerges from water, there is always a storm, and the glare from it is like that of the sun and the moon. It roars like thunder and weighs more than 3,800 catties.
	The Yellow Emperor catches Giant Ox on one occasion, makes a drum from its skin and beats it with the bones of Thunder Beast (Lei Shou 雷獸). The sound can be heard 500 *li* away, filling the world with dread.
Gong Gong 共工	Gong Gong is a god. He has a human face, a snake's body and scarlet hair. He fights with Zhuan Xu 顓頊 to be a *di* 帝 (emperor). He is defeated and becomes so angry that he bumps his head against the Incomplete Mountain and causes one of the pillars supporting the sky to collapse. Thus the sky tilts toward the northwest, where the sun, the moon and the stars converge; the earth crumbles in the south-east, becoming the sea where mud and water flow.
	In ancient China, the title *Gong Gong*, sometimes translated as Common Work, was given to the official in charge of irrigation and water works.
Gou Mang 句芒	See Tree God.
Grow-Back Meat	Shi Rou 視肉. A meat-eating bird with good eyesight.

	Some say that Shi Rou's body is shapeless like a piece of meat. It has no limbs and only a pair of small eyes. If its flesh is cut off and eaten, it will grow back again.
	In the play Shi Rou is a kind of meat.
Gun 鲧	Gun is chief of one of the tribes, later recommended for flood control during the reign of Yao 尧. He tries to contain the water by constructing dikes and embankments, which proves unsuccessful even after nine years at the task. For his failure he is executed by Yao on Feather Mountain 羽山.
	It is said that when he dies, his body does not decompose for three years. The Heavenly Emperor gives orders to cut open Gun's stomach with a Wu knife 吴刀, and out comes a yellow bear, which turns out to be none other than Yu 禹. Yu continues his father's work and finally accomplishes what his father failed to do—controlling the flood—after thirteen years.
He Bo 河伯	See River Lord.
Headless the Reckless	Xing Tian 刑天. Also written as 形天. Headless the Reckless used to have a head. When he fights with the Great God for the control of Heaven, his head is cut off and buried on Chang Yang Mountain. He then uses his nipples as eyes and his navel as a mouth, and holding a shield in his left hand and a battle-axe in his right, he continues to fight and dance at will. He has since been eulogized for his defiant spirit and unyielding will power.
Hiker	Shu Hai 竖亥. A hiker with lots of energy. The highest deity (some claim it to be Yu 禹) orders him to measure the earth by walking. He walks from the easternmost to the westernmost point, and the total number of paces he walks amounts to 500,109,800. From north to

	south, it is 200,033,575 paces. When he hikes, he holds a calculating machine in his right hand and his left hand points north of Mountain Blue 青丘.
Hou Tu 后土	See Earth God.
Incomplete Mountain	Bu Zhou Zhi Shan 不周之山. There is a gap on the northwest side of this mountain where the wind blows through, which accounts for its name *bu zhou* (incomplete).
	On the mountain, there is an excellent fruit tree. Its fruit is like a peach, its leaves are like the jujube's and it has yellow blossoms with a scarlet calyx. Eating the fruit prevents depression.
Jade Grass	Yao Cao 瑤草. The leaves of this plant grow thickly and its flowers are yellow. Anyone who eats it becomes very attractive sexually.
Jie Xiong Guo 結胸國	See Protruding Chest Country.
Jing Wei 精衛	See Dolly.
Jiu Wei Hu 九尾狐	See Nine-Tailed Fox.
Jiu Ying 九嬰	See Nine-Headed Monster.
Junzi Guo 君子國	See Gentlemen Country.
Kai Ming Shou 開明獸	See Bright Beast.
Kua Fu 夸父	See Big Talk.
Kui Niu 夔牛	See Giant Ox.
Lei Shou 雷獸	See Thunder Beast.
Li 櫟	A bird resembling a quail, with black stripes and a scarlet ruff, eaten to cure piles.

Long Snake	Xiu She 修蛇. Long Snake has hair like a pig's mane and makes sounds like drums and wooden clappers.

The story about how Yi the Archer overcomes Long Snake goes like this:

Yi decides to travel to Dongting Lake 洞庭湖 in the south, where a snake has been stirring up trouble. It has overturned many boats and swallowed many fishermen alive. Yi rows a small boat across the lake to search for Long Snake. At the center of the lake he sees the snake raising its head and sticking out its tongue. Big waves are sent surging toward Yi's boat. Immediately, Yi trains his bow on the snake and shoots several arrows in quick succession. Although each arrow hits its vulnerable point, the snake does not die but continues coming steadily toward Yi's boat. Yi takes out his double-edged sword and fights the snake amidst white capped waves which reach to the sky. Finally he manages to cut the snake into several sections and its stinking red blood stains the water of the entire lake. Fishermen on the shore greet Yi with loud cheers as he returns in triumph. |
| Long-Life Hemp | Shou Ma 壽麻. On one occasion, Long-Life Hemp's hometown is in danger of being submerged by the sea. Sensing the perils he leads his family, relatives, neighbors and friends to escape and they are saved. Later he is chosen by the people to become their ruler and the place is known as Shou Ma Country. It is extremely hot in Shou Ma Country. At noon, people stand under the sun but throw no shadows; and when they shout there are no sounds. |
| Moon Mother | Chang Yi 常儀. Also known as Chang Xi 常義. Wife of the Able Emperor and mother of the moon. Some later texts associate her with Chang E. |

Nine-Headed Monster	Jiu Ying 九嬰. A monster spirit which can spurt fire and water.
Nine-Tailed Fox	Jiu Wei Hu 九尾狐. The Nine-Tailed Fox is a man-eater. It has nine tails and makes a sound like a baby. Anyone who eats it will be protected against insect poisoning.
	It is also generally considered an auspicious omen that appears in time of peace.
	Yu 禹 encounters a white Nine-Tailed Fox on Muddy Mountain and considers it an auspicious sign that he will marry the girl of the mountain Pretty Maid.
Nü Jiao 女嬌	See Pretty Maid.
Nü Wa 女娃	See Dolly.
Nü Wa 女媧	The creator of mankind in Chinese mythology. It is said that she copulates with her brother Fu Xi 伏羲 and begets humans. She also uses yellow earth to make men and women, melts stones of five colors to mend a hole in the sky, and snaps off the feet of a giant sea turtle to use as pillars to support the four corners of the sky. She also controls flood water and kills monstrous beasts which harm and terrorize people. As a result of her efforts, the people are able to live peacefully and happily.
Phoenixes and Wonder Birds	Feng Huang Luan Niao 鳳凰鸞鳥. Pheasant-like birds with long tails and five-colored markings. These birds wear snakes on their heads, tread snakes underfoot and wear scarlet snakes on their breasts. They are an omen of world peace. Later they become imperial symbols and a popular motif denoting conjugal harmony.
Pretty Maid	Nü Jiao 女嬌. A famous beauty and wife of Yu 禹. She is a paragon of wifely virtues—after she gets married

	she still yearns for her parents and longs to see them; she does not complain even when her husband Yu refuses to go home for thirteen years for fear that he might be distracted from his flood control responsibilities. Nü Jiao gives birth to Qi 啟, who later becomes the first emperor of the Xia 夏 dynasty.
Protruding Chest Country	Jie Xiong Guo 結胸國. A country in the southwest where people have bulging chests like chicken's breasts.
Qi She Guo 歧舌國	See Reversed Tongue Country.
Qiong Qi 窮奇	See Weird Beast.
Queen Mother of the West	Xi Wang Mu 西王母. Queen of all female deities. She lives on Jade Mountain 玉山, north of the Kun Lun Mountains 崑崙山. She looks like a human but has a leopard's tail and a tiger's teeth, and is good at screaming. In her tangled hair she wears a jade hairpin. To the south are three green birds that bring food to her.
	Book XVI of *The Classic of Mountains and Seas* 山海經 says: "South of the West Sea 西海, on the edge of flowing sands, behind the Red River 赤水, in front of the Black River 黑水, is a big mountain range called the Kun Lun Mountains. There is a spirit with a human face, a tiger's body, stripes and a tail with white spots. Below, Weak River Pool 弱水之淵 surrounds the place. Beyond is Flaming Fire Mountain 炎火之山. Anything thrown in there will immediately burst into flame. There is someone who wears a woman's head ornament, with the teeth of a tiger and a leopard's tail, who lives in a den. She is called the Queen Mother of the West. This mountain has everything."
Ran Yi Fish 冉遺魚	Ran Yi Fish has a fish's body, a snake's head and six feet, with eyes resembling a horse's ears. It has the

	ability to ward off danger and misfortune. After eating a Ran Yi Fish, people will not be blinded by dusts or be afraid of having dreams.
Reversed Tongue Country	Qi She Guo 歧舌國. Literally "Forked Tongue Country." A country in the south where people have tongues rooted at the front of their mouths with the tips pointing toward the throat. This accounts for their name. In some ancient texts, the words *qi she* 歧舌 means "reversed tongue," not "forked tongue." The language of the people in Reversed Tongue Country cannot be understood by foreigners, but the people there understand each other perfectly.
River Lord	He Bo 河伯. The Lord of the Yellow River. He sometimes transforms himself into a white dragon and swims in the river water. Yi the Archer shoots an arrow at him and injures his left eye. As the personification of the power of the Yellow River, the River Lord is often given an unpredictable and demonic character in many stories associated with him. He usually demands young girls as sacrifices; otherwise he will become angry and drown people in the river.
Ru Shou 蓐收	See Autumn God.
Shao Hao 少昊	Descendant of the Yellow Emperor 黃帝 and one of the five *di* 帝 (emperors). He is the chief of the Eastern Yi 東夷 tribe, which adopts birds as their totems. He uses birds' names as the titles of his officials and establishes offices in charge of handicrafts and agriculture. He is also famous for his expertise in irrigation and farming. He sets up his capital at Qufu 曲阜 in Shandong province, which now houses his pyramid-shaped mausoleum.

	In the play Shao Hao is also referred to as the God of Rosy Clouds.
Shen Tu 神荼 and Yu Lei 鬱壘	Shen Tu and Yu Lei are brothers. They are excellent ghost-catchers. Whenever ghosts appear to harass people, they will catch them, tie them up and feed them to tigers. People paint pictures of Shen Tu and Yu Lei which they hang on their front doors to ward off ghosts and evil spirits. Shen Tu is usually painted with a happy white face, while Yu Lei is pictured as having an angry red face.
Shi Rou 視肉	See Grow-Back Meat.
Shi Wu 十巫	See Ten Women Shamans.
Shou Ma 壽麻	See Long-Life Hemp.
Shu Hai 豎亥	See Hiker.
Striped Tree	Wen Jing 文莖. Literally "striped trunk". Its fruit resembles the date and is eaten to cure deafness.
Sun Mother	Xi He 羲和. Wife of the Able Emperor 帝俊 and mother of the sun in Chinese mythology. She often takes a bath at Sweet Spring 甘泉. Later Xi He is also known as the driver of the sun's carriage.
Ten Women Shamans	Shi Wu 十巫, also known as the Ten Shamans of Soul Mountain 靈山十巫. There are reportedly a hundred medicinal herbs to be found on Soul Mountain. The shamans are all outstanding doctors. They ascend to the sky and come down from Soul Mountain, where they gather all kinds of medicine. Some texts claim that the Ten Shamans are actually the ten fingers of Fu Xi 伏羲, the inventor god, and that they have been given godly powers.
Thunder Beast	Lei Shou 雷獸. Thunder Beast has a dragon's body, a human face and a bulging belly. He resides in Thunder

	Marsh 雷澤. Thunder occurs whenever his belly swells.
Tong Qu 鶬渠	See Wagtail.
Torch Dragon	Zhu Long 燭龍. In *The Classic of Mountains and Seas*, it is written: "Beyond the Northwest Sea and north of Red River, there lies the Zhang Wei Mountain 章尾山. On the mountain, there is a red spirit with a human face and a snake's body. His eyes are vertical and the eyelids are straight lines. When he closes his eyes, there is darkness; when he opens his eyes, there is light. He does not eat, sleep or breathe. He can summon the wind and rain, and light up nine levels of shadiness in the underworld."
Tree God	Gou Mang 句芒. A deity in the east with a bird's body and a human face who rides on two dragons.
Tuo Fei 橐𪈘	A bird which looks like an owl, which appears in the winter and hides in the summer. It has a human face but only one foot. Wearing its feathers allays one's fear of thunder and disasters.
Wagtail	Tong Qu 鶬渠. A bird which looks like a pheasant, with a black body and red feet. Eating the Wagtail is an effective way of preventing wrinkles.
Weird Beast	Qiong Qi 窮奇. A monster which looks like a tiger but has wings. He eats people with flowing hair, starting with the head.
Wen Jing 文莖	See Striped Tree.
Windshield	Fang Feng Shi 防風氏. The chief of an ancient tribe. It is said that during the Xia 夏 dynasty, Yu 禹 orders all the divinities to assemble on Mount Huiji 會稽. Windshield arrives late and Yu has him executed.
Winged Dragon	Ying Long 應龍. Winged Dragon has wings on his back.

	This divine creature assists the Yellow Emperor 黃帝 in his battles with other gods. Winged Dragon can withhold rain to cause droughts or cause heavy rainfall to create floods. His biggest accomplishment is to help Yellow Emperor defeat Chi You 蚩尤 and Big Talk. After the battle, Winged Dragon has exhausted all his power and strength and is unable to fly back up to Heaven, hence he moves to the south. That is why the south is often rainy.
Wu Cai Niao 五采鳥	See Five-Colored Birds.
Wu Dao 吳刀	See Wu the Knife.
Wu the Knife	Wu Dao 吳刀. Wu 吳 is a place famous for the making of knives and scissors. When Gun 鯀 dies, his body does not decay for three years. When it is cut open with a Wu Knife, a yellow bear emerges. Some texts claim that it is Yu 禹 who is in Gun's stomach.
	Wu Knife is made into a character called Wu the Knife in the play.
Xi He 羲和	See Sun Mother.
Xi Rang 息壤	See Ever-growing Soil.
Xi Wang Mu 西王母	See Queen Mother of the West.
Xuan Yuan Huang Di 軒轅黃帝	See Yellow Emperor.
Xiang Liu 相柳	See Aide Willow.
Xing Tian 刑天	See Headless the Reckless.
Xiu She 修蛇	See Long Snake.
Ya Yu 猰貐	Also written as 窫窳. A polymorphic creature that feeds

	on humans. It looks like an ox and has a scarlet body, a human face and a horse's feet. It makes a noise like a baby.
Yan Di 炎帝	See Flame Emperor.
Yao Cao 瑤草	See Jade Grass.
Yellow Emperor	Xuan Yuan Huang Di 軒轅黃帝. Revered as the forefather of the Han Chinese race and the builder of the Chinese nation. He was born on the Xuan Yuan Mountain 軒轅山 where the earth is yellow, so he is called the Yellow Emperor of Xuan Yuan.
	He defeats the Flame Emperor and Chi You 蚩尤 in the famous Battle of Zhuo Lu. After he becomes the ruler of China, he then orders his ministers to establish the calendar, writing, music, mathematics and medicine systems. His wife invents silk and a dress code is established. Chinese culture and civilization gradually evolve under his rule.
Yi the Archer	Hou Yi 后羿. An officer in charge of archery during the Able Emperor's reign. He is Chang E's husband, famous for shooting down nine of the ten suns which parch the earth.
Ying Long 應龍	See Winged Dragon.
You Du 幽都	See Death City.
Yu 禹	Also known as Da Yu 大禹 or Xia Yu 夏禹. He is a legendary ruler and king. The son of Gun 鯀, who was executed by Shun 舜 for failing to control the flood, he takes over the task and succeeds after thirteen years. During that time, he passes by the front door of his home three times, but each time he refuses to go in to see his wife and family, fearing that his attention might be diverted from his job. Later he is appointed ruler by Shun before the latter dies. Yu's son Qi 啟 ("open")

	succeeds him as ruler and begins the Xia 夏 dynasty, the first dynasty in Chinese history.
Yu Hao 禺虢	Son of the Yellow Emperor. A sea spirit which dwells in the East Sea 東海. He has a human face and a bird's body, wears a yellow snake in each ear and treads two more yellow snakes underfoot.
Yu Jing 禺京	Son of Yu Hao 禺虢. Yu Hao lives in the East Sea and Yu Jing lives in the North Sea. They are sea spirits.
Yu Mountain 羽山	See Feather Mountain.
Zao Chi 鑿齒	See Chiseled Teeth.
Zhu Long 燭龍	See Torch Dragon.
Zhu Rong 祝融	See Fire God.
Zhuan Xu 顓頊	One of the five emperors in ancient history. Legend has it that Zhuan Xu is the great grandson of the Yellow Emperor. He defeats Gong Gong 共工 and consolidates his rule over the Xia 夏 and the Eastern Yi 東夷 tribes. A quiet, learned and judicious ruler, he promotes economic activities, devises the lunar calendar (the 360-day year) and establishes codes of conduct for the people.

Also referred to as Black Emperor in the play. |